Gospel Life Together

How C.R.O.S.S. Community Can Change Your Life

C.R.O.S.S. Discipleship Community involves
intentionally Gospelling life with others
through focused discussions about one another's
Relational, Personal, Missional, and Spiritual life.

Sandals in Sand
COMMUNICATIONS, LLC.

P.O. Box 3284 • Alpharetta, GA 30023

Thanks to Greg, Shaun, and Perry. Also thanks to Pastor Jason Mather and the congregation of Kings Church, Long Beach, CA. And to my friend and colleague David Whitehead, for his loving and constant challenge to get this done.

Contents

Introduction

"Who spoke and made the sunrise, to light up the very first day?
Who breathed across the water, to start up the very first wave?
It was You.
You introduced Your glory to every living creature on earth.
And they started singing the first song to ever be heard.
They sang for You.
You make all things new. You make all things new.
But then the world was broken, fallen and battered and scarred.
You took the hopeless, the life wasted, ruined and marred...
and made it new.
You make all things new. You make all things new.
You redeem and You transform. You renew and You restore.
You make all things new. You make all things new.
And forever we will watch and worship You!"

"All Things New," Steven Curtis Chapman

I have been a disciple of Jesus Christ for a very long time. I was singing "This little light of mine, I'm gonna let it shine" long before I even had a little light. My conversion experience was at a campfire talk alongside the shoreline of Lake Winnipesaukee, New Hampshire. The reality is I do not remember a time in my life when Jesus wasn't around. Yet, "On my road to righteousness, sometimes the climb has been so steep, I have faltered in my step, but never beyond His reach" (Thanks to Rich Mullins for these words).

I became a disciple, not when I joined a discipleship group in high school, but when I first trusted Christ and turned away from self-salvation at that campfire. Even as a child, I had developed a system for making myself right that needed a deathblow.

Most of my early journey was in a formulaic curriculum approach to growing as a follower of Jesus. We had little books that had a lesson and Bible verses that we were to look up during the week. We then filled in the blank spaces in the book and when we got back together each took a turn offering our answers. We were given Bible verses to memorize and then recite to one another at our weekly meetings. It was intentional, but it was knowledge-based instruction. We were told to just say "no" to our sinful desires.

The assumption was that we would sin less, become "more like Jesus," and become better Christians all by getting the right information, the right answers, and applying them to our will. In many respects, I am grateful for the deep roots and strong foundation I received in Bible memory and theological soundness; but something was lacking.

My adult career has been in the ministry of the local church. I was a youth pastor after college. I have file folders of the materials I used to try and make those teens into faithful followers of Jesus. It was similar to my growing experience. I gave them lots of handouts and fill-in-the-blank type material. I had them read a lot of books. Some of them continued on in faith and others dropped out a long time ago.

My college and theological grad school training at Seminary shared a similar approach. We were given deeper information, challenging memorization, and more doctrine. In my first leadership role as a pastor I defaulted to a para-church ministry's pre-packaged curriculum for disciple-making.

My second church allowed me the opportunity to rethink and re-approach how we were making men and women into followers of Jesus. I realized if we did not get down into their lives at the things that were really controlling or driving them the things they were really living for — despite singing songs that Jesus was all they needed — their lives would never be deeply transformed into all God planned for them, even before the beginning of time (See Ephesians 1:3,4).

As I write this book two events have been in the news cycle. One, a crazed killer entered a college classroom and lined up the students and executed all who claimed to be Christians. The bravest in town that day were the students, from the second and third, all the way to the tenth, who answered "yes" to his question.

The second was a story of a 12-year-old boy and his 41-year-old father who had found Christ as Savior in a foreign country. When radicals ordered them to renounce their newly-found faith in Christ they admitted they could not because of the love He had showed them. They were crucified and beheaded. Both stories expressed a devoted discipleship that is wanting in most contemporary evangelical churches in North America. It challenges even me, and I have "Mastered the Divine" from an accredited seminary.

Jesus called men and women to follow Him. Those who did follow He called His disciples. Of course He had 12 Apostles who were also disciples, but not all of His disciples were Apostles. Jesus said those who followed His commands were His disciples.

Disciples were first called "Christians" in the multi-ethnic church at Antioch (in present day Syria), about 10 years after Jesus returned to the Father (Acts 11:26). We are not certain they meant it in a good way, but up until that time they had been called "People of the Way" (Jesus said He was the Way), or "Nazarenes"(Jesus was from Nazareth), "Galileans" (Jesus was from Galilee and many of the 12 were also), or "Jessaeans" (from the Davidic line of Jesse).

Today, being a disciple of Jesus is called many things. Most people in the Christian community understand it to mean being a follower of Jesus. Some have said it means shaping life to be like Jesus and doing what Jesus said to do. Others have commented that being a disciple simply means being a learner of Jesus.

Definitions are important, because they shape the aim of the heart and life. I like Steve Smallman's definition: "A disciple of Jesus is one who has heard the call of Jesus and has responded by repenting, believing the gospel and following Jesus" ("*The Walk*" p. 26).

Most of my life being "in discipleship" was meant for the fully devoted or for those who wanted to go deeper in the Christian life. It most definitely was for those interested in church leadership. We've been taught that, as the first step, we "accept Jesus as our savior." Then, if you want to go deeper, you might want to be discipled.

However, a believer in Jesus is a disciple. That is the common term: "In Antioch, the *disciples* were first called Christians..." (Acts 11:26 emphasis mine, as noted above). Let me repeat our definition: A disciple is someone who has heard the call of Jesus and responds with repentance, (we will explore this later, but for now it means at the very core, a turning away from any sense of self-saving strategies) believing the gospel, (we will explore this more fully later) and following Jesus (this involves generous obedience in worship, community and mission).

Certainly there are different stages in discipleship. In his works, John Newton (1725-1807) suggested there are basically three stages: New Converts are enthusiastic and zealous for their new-found faith, but often are prone to pride and anxiety because they still have a basic legalism in their Christianity. I have seen that in so many new Christians. They are exuberant (and sometimes obnoxious) about their newly-found forgiveness but base their relationship with God mainly on how well they have abandoned their old sinful lifestyle.

Next are Growing Christians, who through troubles and struggles become more aware of their self-righteousness and deep resistance to the Gospel of grace. Many in North American churches are in this stage. They know they need to keep on keepin' on, but — because of hardships, illness, financial strains or family problems — have actually come to a place of resistance to God and His Spirit.

They wrongly believed that being a Christian should make life get better. When things get harder or life gets busy they tend to get frustrated or angry with God because God is not keeping up His part of the arrangement. They wrongly assume their new life should not be filled with so many struggles or pain.

The third stage is the maturing Christian who can live out Gospel reality not just in crisis but also in everyday life (adapted from Redeemer Presbyterian Church, School of Servant Leadership, version 2.0 1996). We don't use the gospel on the issues of life as if it were a mathematical formula. The Good News is not a principle to master or procedures to follow.

The gospel is power and it is life. It is how we live life as a believer. It is how we relate to ourselves, to God, and to each other. God put it like this: "The just shall live by faith." (Hab. 2:4; Rom. 1:17; Gal. 3:11; Heb. 10:38) The True Christian not only gets in by faith, but also lives only by faith. It is from first to last the way of life.

Many disciple-making systems have defined discipleship as the process of transformation that changes us to be increasingly more like Christ or some similar variation. Disciples are seen as learners of Jesus' teachings, doing what Jesus did, or joining him in mission, etc.

When I hear those types of definitions I hear an overly spiritual type of religion. How are we to be like Jesus? Are we to be God? Are we to do miracles or all become teachers? It's not wrong per se; it just doesn't go far enough. It is "Christianese" or Christian-speak, without explanation. I think, right or wrong, it is turning followers away from, well, following Jesus. It suggests we must strive to do for God and try harder to be like Jesus.

Eugene Peterson explains: "It seems odd to have to say so, but too much religion is a bad thing. We can't get too much of God, can't get too much faith and obedience, can't get too much love and worship. But religion — the well intentioned efforts we make to 'get it all together' for God — can very well get in the way of what God is doing for us. The main and central action is everywhere and always what God has done, is doing and will do for us. Jesus is the revelation of that action. Our main and central task is to live in responsive obedience to God's action revealed in Jesus. Our part in the action is the act of faith" (*"The Message"*, Introduction to Hebrews).

God's intention in making us like Christ is to be as He is, the perfect human. His desire is for you to be fully human in the image of God. Jesus became in human flesh what we were made to be. You becoming like Him is for you to become what God destined, in His original design, for you to be. God made you uniquely you.

Religion always starts with what one has to do to get God or become like God. The gospel of Jesus Christ is that He has already done it, is doing it and will do it. It is all that God has done to get you and remake you into his image; a perfect human (not God).

My father has always loved airplanes and flying. When he turned 18 he joined the Army Air Forces (now the USAF) and became a Sergeant, serving in (among other places) Italy and North Africa during World War II. Many years later, he got his private pilot's license and for a couple of years owned a little Piper Tri-Pacer. He sold that plane and eventually bought a shell of a plane to rebuild.

When I moved him into an assisted living facility, my wife and I ended up throwing away several decades of airplane magazines. He had a passion for flying and for airplanes that I never shared. I dread having to get on another airplane. As father and son we are alike in so many ways, yet, he and I are very unique.

You see, there is no one else with your DNA, both physically and in personality. Your talents, passions, brainpower, creativity, physical presence, beauty, body frame, hairline (or lack of one!) reasoning skill, knowledge base, relational coherence, all make for one profoundly unique and unordinary person. God made you, YOU. I am not my dad, nor do I expect my kids to be me. They are unique and made for a unique purpose.

Yes, we know we are not all that we are supposed to be. That is for God to redeem, restore, and renew. To me that is what it means to be made into the true image of our Maker, Jesus Christ. He will make all things as they are meant to be. However, begin with the reality that you bear the image of God. Essentially, this is what it means for us to be His disciples and to make other disciples — to be shaped into what we were creatively designed to be through gospel renewal and restoration so that ultimately God receives glory.

During the past decade, I have heard hundreds of pastors and leaders express a common theme: "How do we disciple 21st century Christians who live fractured, hurried, and almost frantic lives?" Modern people have busy schedules, travel, work, kids and recreation, and seem barely able to make it to a weekly church service more than two times a month.

In our Gospel-Coaching ministry with new churches (cmmnet.org), disciple-making is always in the top three critical goals church leaders are struggling to implement. Part of the struggle is that many lack a reference point because they themselves have never experienced being discipled. Another struggle is that many leaders refuse to have anything to do with a formulaic approach to discipleship. I get that. We were meant to be a part of a community, sharing life. Not simply "studying" for answers. The gospel is active and the life of the Spirit offers this to us.

Gospelling is the present participle of the word gospel. It means that the good news of Jesus Christ is active now, presently in life, not simply something that occurred in the past. It is the process of how the gospel ignites the relational, personal, missional and spiritual life of the disciple actively and presently.

We are called to enjoy life with God and others because the One who made us receives glory by it. That is the ultimate promise of living life together. My early efforts in making disciples missed the point, focusing mostly on others accepting Christ as Savior and then working on Christian conformity.

Nate Pyle says, "Most people think of the Gospel as a noun. It is a thing. You hear about it. You receive it. You believe it. You share it. The Gospel is something you can hold on to, put in your pocket for another day, or give away. But in 1 Corinthians 15:1, Paul makes a very interesting statement. The NIV translation simply says, "I want to remind you of the Gospel I preached to you…" Nothing interesting there, but the Greek is quite different. The literal Greek translation of this phrase is, 'I want to remind you of the **"Gospel I Gospelled."**

"Gospel" in this case, is both a noun *and* a verb. Not only is it a thing, but it is also something you do. Something you live. Something you embody. You "Gospel."

The point of "Gospelling Life Together" involves intentionally Gospelling life with others through focused discussions about one another's Relational, Personal, Missional and Spiritual life, in the context of regular ongoing friendship for a joyful personal revolution that leads to deeper community and God-honoring, Jesus-glorifying mission in this runaway world. It will happen best when you invite two or three other people into a community of friendship with you and begin a journey together.

I have found — after years of being involved in the lives of thousands of people both as a pastor and Gospel Coach — that most people share similar life questions. They are profound, core or heart kinds of questions that people continually ask themselves.

Sometimes, in the cool of the evening or from a bar stool in a sweaty pub, they might voice them out loud. I suspect you share one or more of the following core life questions regarding your Relational life: "Do people like me for who I am or for what I have? Will I find love in this life? How can I protect myself from pain or rejection?"

Also questions about your Personal life: "Why do I fail at everything I try to do? Am I attractive? Do I have what it takes? How can I make my future secure?"

Regarding your Missional life: "How can I be useful in life? Is this job all I have? How can I make my life make a real difference in the world? How do I talk about God in our godless world?"

And lastly, the Spiritual aspect of life: "Is there a God and is He safe? Does God approve of me? Does He like me? How can I find peace?" I am certain you have asked or still ask one or more of those.

C.R.O.S.S. Community is about the friendship of dialoguing about those types of profound life questions. "Gospelling Life Together" is a journey of laughing and lamenting with a couple of other travellers or disciples. It is praying with and for one another. It is listening and learning one another's life story, enjoying their company and friendship, and progressing forward in the mission God has for each. Why shouldn't our disciple-making relationships be fun?

Shouldn't we play together, tell good jokes, and enjoy life? We must also enter into the sorrow and brokenness of life. We listen to one another's confession of sin and how it has ruined and alienated. We encourage one another back to the Gospel Story of Rescue and Renewal. We are peacemakers. We are participants in Christ's reconciling all things to Himself by sharing the gospel story with those who have not heard His good news.

If you have been part of a discipleship group or in a one-on-one relationship that was focused on your moral conformity or changing your behavior; or simply adding more bible knowledge, rather than having a supernaturally changed life, it may have been helpful and meaningful, but it wasn't Christianity; it was religion. And I suspect it loaded you down with either a lot of pride (you memorized and had the right answers or finally got your act together) or a lot of anxiety (you never seemed to get the right answers or measure up). I hope you will read on and invite two to three others to join you in a new journey of "Gospelling Life Together."

One of my personal core values is Influence. Each week I pray that value into my life. I try to make decisions on the use of my time, my teaching opportunities, and my coaching clients based on influence. Where will I have opportunity to influence others with the good news of Jesus Christ's love, forgiveness and life giving power? You multiply your influence of gospel life into the lives of the others in your C.R.O.S.S. community group, and also into the lives of their spouses (if they are married), kids, other members of your church, their co-workers, and city where you live. Where else can you influence that many people with such good news for life? It's a great reason to get into a C.R.O.S.S. community group.

My hope is you will experiment with this as you intentionally enter into one another's gospel story and mix it up Relationally, Personally, Missionally, and Spiritually.

Chapter One

Why We Are

Gospelling Life Together

"I want to make much of You, Jesus.
I want to make much of Your love.
I want to live today to give You the praise that
You alone are so worthy of.
I want to make much of Your mercy, I want to
make much of Your cross.
I give You my life.
Take it and let it be used to make much of You.
And how can I kneel here, and think of the
cross? The thorns and the whip and the nails
and the spear...
The infinite cost to purchase my pardon and
bear all my shame.
To think I have anything worth boasting in,
except for Your name.
Cause I am a sinner, and You are the Savior
and this is Your love, oh God.
Not to make much of me, but to send Your own
Son so that we could make much of You."

"Much of You," Steven Curtis Chapman

Have you ever considered why we need to be making disciples? Your first answer might be, "Well because we are commanded to do so — it's the Great Commission — 'Go and make disciples.'" Some of the earliest materials on making disciples and even current books and blogs on disciple-making make this point as the starter. We are to make Jesus' final command our first work of the Christian's duty, because Jesus said to help others become like Christ.

We do have the commission from Jesus Himself to disciple, and if we had nothing else that should be enough. However, like any other imperative in the Bible, is the command something sufficient to get us to obey? His commission which really is a present active assumption, "As you are going on in life (as you are living your life), disciple the nations (other ethnic people groups)," came after an enormous amount of time, learning, praying, living in community, co-laboring and readiness with the first twelve Apostles (eleven at that point in the story), and seventy others called disciples.

The "Why" behind disciple making isn't just the fact Jesus commanded us, and the motivation is more than a great command we are to obey. It is vitally important that we understand a motivation that will move us to a continued personal commitment as an intentional choice to involve our lives with the lives of others so each of us becomes what God intends.

A Gospel Why

You see, the Why is the good news of the Gospel itself. We disciple one another because God disciples us with and through what Jesus Christ has done and continues to do, beginning with who we were made to be. God relates to us firstly as persons bearing his image. God the Father, Son and Holy Spirit, in love, made us to know him and find our joy and happiness in Him.

We, as image bearers, are made for relationship, companionship and community. "Let us make man in our image", the triune God said. There is an eternal Father, who has been in relationship with his eternal Son, and eternal Spirit, in perfect community. They have loved, communicated, and created. And by being so, God had no need for us, but we have need for Him. We love and long to be loved.

God said, "It is not good for man to be alone," and He made a woman so they could be companions and multiply themselves, building a larger society of humans. There is male and there is female because that is the way God made us; to be in perfect community with one another and with their Father-Son-Spirit Creator Who is community.

We are the completion of His creation and He affirmed it by saying it is "very good." THIS IS GOOD NEWS! We were created by the eternal life-giving God to know Him and find our enjoyment in and with Him. Our lives have purpose. Our lives are going somewhere. Our lives have dignity, beauty, and meaning. Our work and mission have meaning. The very universe has meaning. This is how the story begins. We are the crown of his creation. That is a good thing! (We will consider in more detail the good news and the bad news in chapter 5.)

God is Gospelling Life Together with You

Secondly, we understand that through the generosity of Jesus Christ and the sending of His Spirit, we are being daily Gospelled. God the Son, Jesus Christ personally came, incarnating Himself as a fully-human being. He came to rescue and reconcile to Himself all things; and by His work through his Spirit He daily gives life, serves, and conforms us into the perfect image of God we were meant to be. He started it and he will complete the work He began; daily working in us that we would be completely renewed and part of the renewal of all things (we will consider this in great detail in Chapter 6). We get to share in His ongoing work to rescue this runaway planet because we have been given an ambassadorship by the King!

Jesus Followed the Father

Thirdly, we are motivated to be gospelling life with others because God the Son, Jesus, followed the Father, because all of us refused to follow. Rather than crush our rebellion, Jesus, at great cost, voluntarily humbled Himself and learned obedience through the things He suffered (Hebrews 5:8). Out of the Father's great love for us, He transferred our sin and shame — past, present and future — onto His only Son when He was put to death; punishing Him in our place and removing our guilt and shame.

While we were enemies dishonoring the Father, Jesus the "Firstborn Son" over all things (as the True Obedient Son) became the substitute; covered and healed our shame, so we could become sons and daughters. We are not simply followers, we are sons and daughters of God.

Jesus Called You to Follow Him

Fourthly, a motivation for gospelling life together is that Jesus Christ chose you to be His disciple. When He chose His first twelve disciples it was quite the scandal. In those days the disciple chose his teacher or guide. However, Jesus invited them, "Come follow me and learn from me." It is why later He said to them, "You did not choose me, but I chose you and appointed you so that you might go and bear fruit — fruit that will last." (John 15:16)

He has pursued you and made you His disciple and He continues to disciple you Relationally, Personally, Missionally and Spiritually every day..He is gospelling you moment-by-moment. Knowing we are chosen and are being gospelled by God provides us destiny and hope. You are not alone randomly cruising through this world.

Parents Disciple Their Children

Fifthly, if you are a parent, you already have a God-given joy of gospelling life together with your child or children. You don't have to learn their story as you are a main character in their story and in the shaping of their story. Perhaps one of the reasons many teens "age out" of Christianity or church when they get to college isn't because they were part of a lousy youth group in a small church (as one mega-pastor recently proclaimed) but because Dad and Mom didn't see themselves as disciple-makers, intentionally engaging their kids with focused gospel discussions about their son or daughter's relationships, personal issues, missional calling, and spiritual condition.

Parenting is more than raising our kids to be moral citizens or getting them a good education so they can secure a job with excellent benefits. If that is all you want for your son or daughter (even if they are little tots right now), let me invite you to enlarge your vision for their future.

The Barna Group, a research firm, found, "A person's moral foundations are generally in place by the time they reach age 9. While those foundations are refined and the application of those foundations may shift to some extent as the individual ages, their fundamental perspectives on truth, integrity, meaning, justice, morality and ethics are formed quite early in life. After their first decade,most people simply refine their views as they age without a wholesale change in those leanings."

Furthermore, a person's response to the meaning and personal value of Jesus Christ's life, death, and resurrection is usually determined before a person reaches the age of 18. In fact, a majority of Americans make a lasting determination about the personal significance of Christ's death and resurrection by age 12. Barna research also showed data indicating that in most cases people's spiritual beliefs are irrevocably formed when they are pre-teens (www.barna.com/research). What a grand time we can have with our children.

You Need Community to Change

Sixthly, we come to see the reality that there is no such thing as making it on our own. We learn and change best in community with others. We need others and they need us. The truth is even when you live alone all your annoying habits do not go away. I need to be gospelled by others because I so easily slip into doubt. When Thomas the disciple did not believe Jesus had been raised from the dead (and by the way the other disciples did not believe it either until they had seen Him), it was his community of other disciples who kept saying to him it is true, we have seen Him.

> *"The central work of God's kingdom is change. God accomplishes this work as the Holy Spirit empowers people to bring His Word to others. We bring more than solutions, strategies, principles, and commands. We bring the greatest story ever told, the story of the Redeemer. Our goal is to help one another live with a 'God's story' mentality. Our mission is to teach, admonish, and encourage one another to rest in His sovereignty, rather than establishing our own; to rely on His grace rather than performing on our own; and to submit to His glory rather than seeking our own. This is the work of the kingdom of God; people in the hands of the Redeemer, daily functioning as His tools of lasting change."*
> ("*Instruments in the Redeemer's Hands,*" Paul Tripp)

We have been called to be in a community with other believers. We should dispel the myth that believers do not need to go to church to be Christians. Paul writes, "His intent was that now, through the church, the manifold wisdom of God should be made known to the rulers and authorities in the heavenly realms" (Ephesians 3:10). We, His Church, are a way God works to display His glory in the theater of the universe.

New Models Needed

Seventh, we must grapple with how the emerging generation learns. If we continue trying to deliver a disciple-making program in our churches that does not take note of how millennials have been educated or how they learn they will lose out in growing in their journey to follow Jesus deeply and with devotion.

Most were educated in teams, in community, and experiential learning. Most are motivated to learn what they want to learn, not what they are told they have to learn. They believe that learning is a continuous cycle of information, action and reflection, not simply a transfer of information. They can search the web for information. We learn by connecting new information to what we already know and linking it to personal experience. "We live in a knowledge economy," said Peter Drucker. We can get the knowledge we want through various channels.

Most adults do not want to know more for the sake of knowledge itself. They will be more self-directed, wanting to apply what they know and share it with others in a community that is also learning through experience. They want to be more directly connected to their own development and learning so they can immediately apply those insights to life.

I suspect fewer and fewer younger church members will enroll in formal discipleship courses that are top-down directed with lectures and notebooks or be willing to get teamed up one-on-one with a "Disciple expert" who will transfer knowledge as a superior to an inferior. This is why we need a new approach that helps shape disciples in community with intentionality yet more self-directed.

Summary

We must tap into the gospel motivation of why we are "Gospelling Life Together," be captivated by Him and the implications of all the good news He brings in everyday life. If we are not gospelling life by dealing with the motivational structures of the core of life — if disciples do not get to the thing that is really driving them and functioning as their life operating system — then they are left primarily working by duty and/or feelings in an effort to "just try harder."

We must focus more on being made as an image bearer; being so loved, forgiven, rescued and empowered we can overcome the things in life that work to crush, enslave and kill. We have been given His Holy Spirit for power to change. It is perfect Life on life. He lives now interceding with the Father on our behalf, to love and give mercy, power and purpose. The gospel isn't just to get us forgiven and "saved" for the future but for life now. British Brethren pastor wrote in the late 1800's:

> "We must remember that God will never drag us along the path of true-hearted discipleship. This would greatly lack the moral Excellency which characterizes all the ways of God. He does not drag, but draw us along the path that leads to ineffable blessedness in Himself; and if we do see that it is for our real advantage to break through all the barriers of nature, in order to respond to God's call, we forsake our own mercies. But alas! our hearts little enter into this. We begin to calculate about the sacrifices, the hindrances, and the difficulties, instead of bounding along the path, in eagerness of soul, as knowing and loving the One whose call as sounded in our ears." (C. H. Macintosh)

C.R.O.S.S. Disciple Community involves intentional Gospel conversations with focused discussions about one another's Relational, Personal, Missional and Spiritual life so that each disciple loves, matures and reproduces, by the Spirit's power, the way God intends. It is at a most basic level gospelling life with others where each intends to connect and understand one another's story — their Backstory, how Christ has and is rescuing and discover what mission the Spirit intends for each to be a part in the renewal of all things.

Once we understand the better Why of gospelling life, other than simply another command to follow, our next movement is to see and understand our Core Disciple Identity.

Chapter Two

Why Your Core Matters

"You are the Way, the Truth, and the Life. And You've promised never to leave me. My Savior, my friend, from beginning to end. So where else could I turn? And where else could I go? You have given me life . You have made me whole. You have rescued my soul.So where else could I go? For I am found in You. All I've been made for. So there's no where else I could go. I am found in you."

"I Am Found In You," Steven Curtis Chapman

All the exercise programs out now advocate the necessity for the body having a strong core. It is vital to have a strong foundation for all activities and is essential for your balance, lower back strength, arm and leg motion and practically every movement you make. Higher core strength lowers the risk of injury. Your physical body's core is a stabilizer for how you move. And when it gets out of shape or is neglected, your entire body's health is affected.

Core Disciple Identity is a vital component to living a healthy life. It is more than taking a selfie and posting it on Instagram. I recently saw a young man with a T-shirt that read, "Always be yourself! Unless you can be Batman. Then always be Batman." Have you ever wished you were someone else? Do you know your identity?

Your personal Core Identity is crucial to your life. Everyone operates their life by it; everything from the way they manage stress, make or break relationships, chose a career or what neighborhood to live in. Everyone whether religious or not has a spiritually-based core identity. It is how you have answered two fundamental questions: who am I and why am I here? Where you find your identity determines how you live. There are several typical yet *false approaches* to finding our identity.

"I am who I am connected to."

A lot of people have created the identity they want through their Facebook page and find personal sense of being by the number of friends they have. For others it's the number of followers on their Twitter or Instagram account. When you are asked to introduce yourself what do you say? I suspect you begin with your name and then who you are related to in this world; I am Rachel's husband or sometimes I am Annie's dad, depending on the context. We can seek an identity that is based on our relationships. But being related to someone else can never be the core of who you are.

"I am what I am."

I know several people who think they are who they are because of their physical appearance: great looks or physically fit. Sadly, some find themselves in their intellect or theological prowess. Parents have told their kids, "It doesn't matter what others think of you, what matters is what you think of yourself."

If you have ever had the courage to look at pictures of yourself in middle school you might want to ask your parents "Why did you let me look like that?" The answer probably will be: "You chose to look like that. You were forming your identity."

How you see yourself at 13 is radically different than when you are 25, and then 35. We have a generation of adults who don't know who they are because they were told to look inside themselves for themselves.

"I Am What I Do."

Another way is to develop an identity is based on what we do for living: "Hi, I'm Dr. Tom. I'm President of CMM." Titles, jobs, education or activities are often ways to find our sense of self. A lot of pastor friends I have confess that they have formed their spiritual identity by their ministry. Cultivating their life with God is only found by their ongoing sermon preparation or teaching. Prayer is conducted in public and sounds exceedingly pious and profound. However, their identity "in Christ" is elusive or non-existent. They are professional Christians.

A lot of older, more established religious people tend to find their identity through the things they are doing for God. They tithe, attend church, serve on a committee, and might even give to the building fund. A lot of new Christians find their identity in what they have stopped doing. They no longer get drunk or have slowed down on cursing. They may have stopped sleeping around (at least they are trying). They have cleaned up their act and in so doing think they have a new identity.

Now don't get me wrong — they are still "in Christ." The Apostle Paul went to great lengths in Ephesians to make the point that those who have faith in Christ are now "in Christ." But let's be honest, loads of us no longer form our identity by being "in Christ," but by what we do or don't do. That, my friends, will wear you out.

My friend Dr. John Thomas said once, "Very few Christians know how to solidly appropriate the justifying work of Christ in their lives. Most tend to have such a light view of God's holiness and the depth of their own sin that they see little need for justification, and yet below the surface of their lives they are deeply guilt-ridden and insecure. Instead they tend to rely on their sanctification for their justification. They try to quiet their consciences by their obedience. They draw their assurance of salvation from their sincerity and their past experience of conversion, their recent efforts to obey and the relative absence of conscious, willful, 'big' sins."

The only identity equation that works in God's gospel-Kingdom and leads to a healthy and thriving life is your Core Disciple Identity.

Your CDI **(Core Disciple Identity)** is composed of three parts; not one or two. Your health as a disciple of Jesus is consistent with the degree to which you understand these realities and have integrated these three aspects into your inner being they form a healthy identity. In fact, I'm certain your health and thriveability in your Christian life is related to the degree you have incorporated them into your sense of being. I have to label them as one, two and three, but I do not intend to mean they are ordered in priority. They are interlinking and always being played as one song in perfect harmony in your inner being.

Made, not Self-made

First, God made you and all things for His own glory. You were created by a loving Father who is the Maker of heaven and earth. The Apostles Creed probably originated about 350 years after Jesus walked the earth and is one of the earliest statements of Christian faith. It begins with the words, "I believe in God the Father Almighty, Maker of heaven and earth." Why? I think partly because they understood it as vital to our identity.

The Bible is filled with Psalms, Prayers and direct statements that remind us that God is our loving maker or creator. One example is in Psalm 121 when the writer proclaims,

> *"I lift up my eyes to the mountains — where does my help come from? My help comes from the Lord, the Maker of heaven and earth. He will not let your foot slip — He who watches over you will not slumber; indeed, He who watches over Israel will neither slumber nor sleep. The Lord watches*

*over you—the Lord is your shade at your right hand; the sun
will not harm you by day, nor the moon by night. The Lord
will keep you from all harm — He will watch over your life;
the Lord will watch over your coming and going both now
and forevermore."*

When our daughters were little they struggled at times with
nightmares or fear of the dark. One of the passages they memorized
was Psalm 100. One of the verses encouraged them to "Know that the
LORD is God. It is He who made us, and we are His. We are His
people; the sheep of His pasture." When they were afraid they would
speak to their little hearts that reality. "There is a God who made me
and I am a little sheep under His care."

The Apostle Paul informs the Christians in Colossae, a city with
multiple beliefs about origin:

*"The Son (Jesus Christ) is the image of the invisible God, the
firstborn over all creation. For in Him all things were
created: things in heaven and on earth, visible and invisible,
whether thrones or powers or rulers or authorities; all things
have been created through Him and for Him."* (Col 1:15,16)

The last book of the bible, Revelation, is full of reminders of
God's creative work:

*"Worthy are You, our Lord and our God, to receive glory and
honor and power; for You created all things, and because of Your
will they existed, and were created"* (Rev 4:11).

Does this change the way you see yourself? Unlike other gods in
various religions and myths, God is not a single-person god in search
of creatures to serve Him or in need of love. You do not fill a void that
God had. He does not want to use you for His own service, as if He

needed to be served. We are made in His likeness to enjoy His being in all his glory. You were made to get God, the greatest good in the universe.

Understanding God as our maker helps explain beauty, glory, wonder, awe, creativity, art, color, complexity, order, love, peace, and generosity. It explains the sense of fulfillment when you say, "This is what I was made for!" We will discuss this further in the chapters on knowing the Gospel Story and telling your story. If you want to know God you have to know your story, and if want to know your story you have to know the Gospel Story. And the Backstory of the Gospel Story begins with God making you and all things.

One of the effects of 50 years of our cultural consensus — that there is no Creator, there is only the natural — is an unsettled inner thought world and it affects your identity. It comes as subtly as, "You can be anything you want to be so follow your heart." The false starting point is that you are the "captain of your own soul and life" because there is no Creator and therefore live as if this world is all there is.

Another myth that "you have to be true yourself and follow your dreams" creates pressure on our minds. It says you are self-made and control your own destiny. That is the prevailing consensus in culture, a theme in almost every Hollywood script, every pop song and TV show. We also teach our children these myths and subject them to a natural world, not a supra-natural world where they can find their greatest happiness in the God who made them.

My daughter was teaching her then two-year old son that God had made all things and had made him using a question and answer approach that simply starts, "Who made you?" Response: "God made me." "What else did God make?" Response: "God made all things." "Why did God make you and all things?" Response: "For His own glory."

However, his answer veered off course one morning. To the next question, "What else did God make?" came his response, "Bacon. God made bacon."

It is deeply important to understanding yourself and your identity that you grasp the profound reality that there is a personal God who made you in His image. To add one great twist to that reality is to remember that that God is a Father.

J.I. Packer puts it simply, "What is a Christian?' The question can be answered in many ways, but the richest answer I know is that a Christian is one who has God for his Father'...Our highest privilege and deepest need is to experience the holy God as our loving Father, to approach Him without fear and to be assured of His fatherly care and concern."

Steve Childers is a renowned authority on all things Church Planting, Growth and Renewal. He is a Seminary Professor and President of a cutting edge online training ministry for the nations. In an unpublished paper he wrote,

> *"Since Christ created everything that is and since He is ruling over everything that is, then everything that is must be ultimately directed back to Him. This is why Paul said in I Corinthians 10:31, 'So whether you eat or drink or whatever you do, do it all for the glory of God.' Since Jesus Christ is the First Cause and Supreme Ruler of all things, we must learn to see Him as the Final Cause of everything we do—not just the religious things we do."*

Since God has made you that changes everything about who you are and about the life you live. You were wonderfully made in the image of God and are the very opposite of being self-made or a cosmic accident.

A Contra-Conditional Love that Reconciles

The second part of your CDI is that God has loved and adopted you as His son or daughter. You are a created creature, but at the same time a child of God. God the Father loves you with the same infinite love He loves God the Son, Christ. "For He has rescued us from the dominion of darkness and brought us into the kingdom of the Son He loves, in whom we have redemption, the forgiveness of sins." (Col. 1:13,14)

F.B. Meyer said, "It is ever so sweet to rest on a love which is dated not in time, but eternity. Because one feels that as God's love did not originate in any unforeseen flash of excellence in us, so it will not be turned away by any unexpected outbreak of depravity. It did not begin because of what we were and it will continue in spite of what we are."

Think of all of the realities in the Bible about the fact that those who are sons and daughters of God are deeply loved; "God so loved, He sent His One and Only Son." (John 3:16); "For the Lord is good and His love endures forever." (Psalm 100:5); "In love, he predestined us for adoption to sonship." (Eph. 1:5); "Who loved me and gave himself for me." (Gal.2:20); "The love of Christ (for me) constrains me." (2 Cor. 5:14); "How great the Father's love is for us that we should be called sons/daughters of God. And that is what we are." (I John 3:1);

"I pray that you... may have power...to grasp how wide and long and high and deep is the love of Christ and to know this love."(Eph. 3:18).

Most of us have heard that God loves us unconditionally. We have been told that true love is blind; that God's love is a blind love and He loves you just the way you are. However, love is not blind. True loves sees all, knows all and still loves. There are a few people in this world that love me a lot. Many of my friends basically put up with me but there is one person who loves me the most out of all people — my wife Rachel. Trust me when I say her love for me is not blind. She knows more and sees more than any other human yet her love is deeper and greater than anyone else's.

God's love is not simply an unconditional love. It's not less than that but it's far deeper and greater. God's love is contrary to your condition. David Powilson wrote,

> "God does not accept me just as I am; He loves me despite how I am. He loves me just as Jesus is; He loves me enough to devote my life to renewing me. This love is much, much better than unconditional! Perhaps we could call it 'contra-conditional' love. God has blessed me because His Son fulfilled the conditions I could never achieve. Contrary to what I deserve, He loves me. And now I can begin to change, not to earn love, but because I've already received it."
> ("Seeing with New Eyes")

To the degree the reality of His contra-conditional love (God's love is deeper and grandeur than your condition) gets into your heart or soul to that degree you will discover a motivation for life unlike any other. It will heal the shame from your past. It can take you through your current pain and loss, and the coming persecution for being a disciple of Jesus.

—

We are loved adopted sons and daughters of the One who made us for Himself, for loving others, and for His mission to the nations. In his contra-conditional love he predestined us to be adopted children. J.I. Packer, noted scholar and writer penned in one of his classic works, *"Knowing God"*:

> *"Our first point about adoption is that it is the highest privilege that the Gospel offers: higher than justification ...that justification, by which we mean God's forgiveness of the past together with His acceptance for the future, is the primary and fundamental blessing of the Gospel is not the question...but this is not to say that justification is the highest blessing of the Gospel. Adoption is higher, because of the richer relationship with God that it involves...Justification is a forensic idea, conceived in terms of law, viewing God as judge...justification does not of itself imply any intimate or deep relationship with God the judge...but Adoption is a family idea, conceived in terms of love, and viewing God as father. In adoption, God takes us into His family and fellowship, and establishes us as His children and heirs...to be right with God the judge is a great thing, but to be loved and cared for by God the father is a greater blessing"* (1995).

We were born into this world alienated from God. We added to our ruin by our ongoing doubts and willful choices to run our lives contrary to our design. However, by faith in the life, death, and bodily resurrection of Jesus Christ we are reconciled to God and have been made right with Him, free from any accusation. It is not enough to ask, "Have you made peace with God?" The most important question is, "Has God made peace with you?"

God is no longer angry with you because Christ has made peace with God for you (Col. 1:19-21). That means as God's son or daughter He no longer thinks bad thoughts about you. He has adopted you in as his heir. He closed the gap between God and you.

Many sermons, teachings, and books on being a Christian suggest the core of our identity is the fact that you are perfectly loved and adopted and that progress is made in discipleship by resting in that reality. I heard a lead worshipper in church introduce a song by asking, "What would happen if you truly believed God loved you perfectly as a loved son or daughter?"

It is a wonderful question. Because if we did believe it deep down it would fundamentally affect the way we handle criticism, how we treat other humans despite their race, social class, wealth, or country of origin. We would not be agitated when we are slighted or ignored.

As I pondered his question I asked myself two other questions. What would happen if I truly believed that God made me, that I am not a self-made man, and He is the ruler over me? How would that change the decisions I make? Quite a huge difference I believe.

Our internal song that we were made by a good God and adopted by that good God who is a Father who loves us is now a two-part harmony. Some books on being a follower of Jesus neglect the part of you being created. When you combine those two ideas together it is astonishing and freeing.

In his book "*The Good God,*" Michael Reeves writes, "The most foundational thing in God is not some abstract quality but the fact that He is Father... Since God is before all things a Father, and not primarily Creator or Ruler, all His ways are beautifully fatherly...thus all he does he does as Father. That is who He is. He creates as a Father and he rules as a Father; and that means the way He rules over creation is most unlike any other god would rule over creation."

But there is another third part and it is important that you add this part into your core.

Simul Justus et Peccator

The third part of your CDI is that you are simultaneously a justified saint and a sinner at the same time. You must constantly see yourself moment by moment as a saint/sinner every day. On this side of God renewing all things you will never be more of a saint than you are today. And you will never be less of a sinner.

This doesn't mean that we are Jekyl and Hyde; that one day we act like a sinner and one day a saint. We also are not partial saints and partial sinners as if sometimes I am a good person and sometimes I'm a selfish pig. I am both a good person and a selfish pig in the same moment; just ask my kids.

I wear a ball cap when I am out in the sun since I have a wide part on my head and already had minor skin cancer. To protect myself I bought a cap in St. Thomas, Virgin Islands. My cap says St. Thomas on the front. Of course not everyone gets the irony.

Paul regularly referred to the followers of Jesus as holy saints. We are saints of God, holy and perfect in his sight. I am St. Thomas. When I was a pastor I tried to get my staff to call me St. Thomas, though they never did adopt the title.

Yet we have to be aware of the proclivity we have to doubt God and to disobey what God clearly showed as the way of life. You are still a sinner. Yes, you died to sin in your position with Adam but you are also told to put sin to death (Col. 3:3,5). You are not like a dead body in a casket that is unresponsive to lust, greed and envy. If you are unclear about this reality — that at the same moment you are a saint, positioned in Christ with all his favor and still someone who can walk away in one moment of your choosing — your CDI will be marred. This is the reality of the gospel.

One of the prevailing beliefs of our Western culture is that all of your problems in life are out there somewhere and the solution to them can be found within yourself. We are born basically good and it is the external forces of society or family of origin or poor conditions in early childhood that corrupts us. Gospel Christianity comes along and says the problem you have is inside you. Jesus said, "For it is from within, out of a person's heart, that evil thoughts come: sexual immorality, theft, murder, adultery, greed, malice, deceit, lewdness, envy, slander, arrogance and folly" (Mark 7:21,22).

The Apostle James added years later, "What causes fights and quarrels among you? Don't they come from your desires that battle within you?" (James 4:1). You do not have pure motives nor a selfless inner heart. If we say we do not sin we deceive ourselves.

If you forget or deny you are a sinner you may be devastated by your sinful behavior or the sin of someone else because you have too high a view of self. When you forget you are a saint you live in the shadows naked and afraid having too low a view of self and not remembering that Jesus paid the price to cancel the debt with God and to break the power of sin in life.

We are justified completely yet in and of ourselves we still have sin; we're still sinners. But by faith in Jesus Christ whose righteousness is now transferred to our account we are considered just or right with God. This reality is termed double-imputation. Your sin and shame is imputed to Jesus (put into Jesus's account if you will) and His perfect life and all his "rightness" is imputed to you (put into your life's account). In this two-fold transaction we see that God, who does not negotiate with us over our sin, but rather punished sin fully when He imputed it to Jesus, yet, His righteousness comes to me in the sight of God. Jesus is both the Just One (he didn't overlook my sin) and the Justifier (he paid the price for my sin).

The Apostle Paul described it in 2 Corinthians 5:17-21:

> "Therefore, if anyone is in Christ, the new creation has come: The old has gone, the new is here! All this is from God, who reconciled us to himself through Christ and gave us the ministry of reconciliation: that God was reconciling the world to Himself in Christ, not counting people's sins against them...God made Him who had no sin to be sin for us, so that in Him we might become the righteousness of God."

Author and pastor Tim Keller wrote:

> "The essence of what makes Christianity different from every other religion and form of thought is this: Every other religion says if you want to find God, if you want to improve yourself, if you want to have a higher consciousness, if you want to connect with the divine however it is defined — you have to do something. You have to gather your strength, you have to keep the rules, you have to free your mind, then you have to fill your mind, and you have to be above average. Every other religion or human philosophy says if you want to make the world right, or make yourself right, then summon all your reason and your strength, and live in a certain way. Christianity says the exact opposite. Every other religion...says you have to do something...but Christianity says no, Jesus Christ came to do for you what you couldn't have done for yourself...[religion] says 'Here's what you have to do to find God.' Christianity is about God coming to earth...dying on a cross, to find you" (Encounters with Jesus, 2013).

You see, gospelling life together means we remind one another that Christianity isn't so much about what we have to do for God but we remind each other of what God has done to rescue us to Himself through Jesus. When we remember, we also turn from our self-righting activities and plans. Because we have been so loved by the God who made us we live by the fight of faith that it has all already been done — in generous obedience in our new life and move out in love to tell others how they can find rescue too. Make disciples of others among the nations as you go along. Gospelling life together describes what living as an image bearer looks like; how a son or daughter responds and how a saint's life operates while still being a sinner.

Chapter Three

Realities of a Healthy Core Disciple Identity

"This is the reason we were made.
To know the love of our Creator.
And to give the love He's given us away.
Yeah, the Maker, and the Father, and the God of everything.
He says to love, love, love, cause after all, it's all about love.
Gods says love, love, love, love, love, yeah yeah.
It's all about love, love, love, love, love.
Everything else comes down to this,
nothing any higher on the list than love.
Cause after all, it's all about love."

"It's All About Love," Steven Curtis Chapman

I suspect if you have read this far you are on a journey for personal revolution and yet desire to be connected with others in the journey as well. You might have tried to involve yourself in a study class or getting with a few other men or women to discuss the Bible or Christian book. It has no doubt helped, yet I am under no illusion that you have arrived at a spiritual destination that has made you feel completed. I hope as you discuss in your discipleship community — a group with at least two others — the Core Identity each of you has as a disciple of Jesus. It will enlarge your life and help you gain a greater depth of all it means to be His.

Carol had been raised in the church and had become an extremely talented and competent woman by her mid-twenties. She was determined, disciplined, and dependable. At church, she was also ready to volunteer and serve when asked. By the time she was married and raising a family she began to have serious internal doubts about faith and church. However, because of her disciplined life she hung in. Her husband took a new job and the family moved to a new city where they joined a new church. They both heard a gospel they had never experienced. She was invited by two other women to join a small group and was unprepared for what God had in store.

Carol discovered that all her years of hard work was not because of spiritual character or the fruit of a supernaturally changed heart, but really a drive for personal security. She had used her conformity to the rules and disciplines to keep her life comfortable. When she discovered her Core Identity, and then as the three women continued to deepen their friendship in faith, they began to make sense out of their personal stories, applying the hope of the gospel in every arena. Carol found freedom and an inexpressible song of joy. That joy spread to her home, her friends, and co-workers. She is truly a remarkable woman of grace.

In this chapter I'd like explore the four realities or implications of our true Core Identity; that is the three-part song as a created son or daughter who lives in the here and now as a saint/sinner. As that song is played in your inner being and you hold those three perspectives of your identity in harmony it takes you somewhere. And the Bible is clear that having a clear identity moves us Relationally, Personally, Missionally, and Spiritually. It has a full-orbed effect on life.

The Relational Aspect

First, in regards to the relational aspect of your new life, you were made for and adopted into Community. God is a community as Father, Son, and Spirit and has been eternally expressing His love. The movement in all Christian discipleship is "Faith expressing itself in love" (Gal. 5:6).

The New Testament uses "One another" 100 times in 94 different verses. We are to be "one-anothering" as disciples of Jesus. For instance we are to "one another" in love (forgiving, not judging, speaking truth), in humility (preferring, submitting, giving deference to) and in serving (hospitality, washing feet, encouraging). Why? Paul makes the case when he wrote to the disciples in the church at Ephesus. "As deeply loved children *live a life of love (emphasis added)*, just as Christ also loved us and gave Himself up for us...as a sacrifice..." (My translation).

The fact that God in Christ loved us, gave Himself for us, and adopted us as His very own (the gospel as good news) has a resultant reality for His disciple: The new mark of a Christian is love. We are not expected to be co-creators of new worlds or new animals. We are to follow His example of love for others in community.

> *"What then shall we conclude but that as the Samaritan loved the wounded man, we as Christians are called upon to love all men as neighbors, loving them as ourselves. Second, that we are to love all true Christian brothers in a way that the world may observe. This means showing love to our brothers in the midst of our differences – great or small – loving our brothers when it costs us something, loving them even under times of tremendous emotional tension, loving in a way the world can see.... Love – and the unity it attests to – is the mark Christ gave Christians to wear before the world...With this mark the world will know that Christians are indeed Christians and that Jesus was sent by the Father."* ("*True Spirituality*", Francis Schaeffer)

Jesus said, "A new command I give you, 'Love one another. As I have loved you, so you must love one another'" (John 13:34). He added, "By this others will know you are my disciples... If you read the bible, go to a bible study, pray before meals, have a 'God is my Co-pilot' bumper sticker, and send your kids to Christian school." Ok, that's not what He said. What Jesus did say was that we have to love from the heart.

The Personal Aspect

Second, the effect the gospel has on the Personal aspect of your Core Identity is that you are no longer your own. Paul informs us via his letter to the disciples in Corinth, "You are not your own; you were bought at a price. Therefore honor God with your bodies" (I Corinthians 6:19).

Todd has been a friend for over fifteen years. He has been an elder in several churches over the span of his 50 plus years on this earth. He has taught bible studies, shared his faith in Christ, been on mission trips with his church, and even helped start a church or two.

One morning over scrambled eggs and bagels he said, "I'm not sure I believe this stuff anymore. I mean I've been burned by pastors and churches and don't see how God is changing anyone, including me. I am adrift and quit going to church several months ago."

I felt his internal pain and knew of his hard life. His Backstory is amazingly brutal. The fact that he had followed Jesus for so many years so faithfully was inspiring. I only had one response. I asked a question.

"Todd, do you think you will thrive in life finding absolute joy in being your own master? If so, go for it." He called me a very bad name.

Before Christ bought you, you were in Adam. He rebelled and brought ruin, alienation and death. You were born into spiritual ruin/alienation/death and were a slave to sin and its desires. You controlled nothing in your destiny. Death was your destiny and there was nothing you could do to stop that fate. God's curse was upon you.

When Christ came and died on the cross in your place who you were in Adam, your legal standing with God, and the universe died. And when Jesus was raised to new life you, in union with Him, you were raised too. His resurrection is your resurrection to life. You have now been reconciled to God and have peace with God because

Jesus bought you by His own blood (His death) and have been raised to life. It is all by His grace and grace alone; nothing in what you did or tried to do, no matter how kind your intentions. Our only contribution to our salvation was the sin and shame that made His substitute necessary.

Now you are "In Christ." You are freed from your enslavement but you are not your own property to do with as you wish. It is because the Gospel is by sheer grace not by any works of your own means there isn't anything God can't ask of you. You belong to Christ, body and soul.

In 1562, a group of Christians began using a learning tool called a *Catechism* to teach their own hearts and minds as well as their children and other members the basic fundamentals of Christianity. It was a gospel tool and still is. One of the statements declared:

"I am not my own, but belong body and soul, both in life and in death, to my faithful Savior Jesus Christ. He has fully paid for all my sins with His precious blood, and has set me free from all the power of the devil. He also preserves me in such a way that without the will of my heavenly Father not a hair can fall from my head; indeed, all things must work together for my salvation. Therefore, by His Holy Spirit he also assures me of eternal life and makes me heartily willing and ready from now on to live for him." (Heidelberg Catechism Q&A 1)

We now build life around Christ alone because His Righteousness has been put into our lives. We have a new identity and new desires and affections. Christ is in you. He has clothed you with Himself, removed your personal shame and all its destructive results. You are free because you are bought with His life, death, and resurrection.

There is no shame. There is nothing to prove, nothing to fear and nothing to hide. And you are His very own.

When Paul informed the disciples in Corinth of this reality he applied it directly to an area that was part of their immediate culture — sex. He said in effect, "Your body isn't yours to do with as you want any more. You cannot use your body for sex with anyone you want.

Part of the reason he had to explain it to them was in their culture sex was rampant and hardly anyone believed it to be morally wrong. In fact, the religious temples used sex and the sex trade as a means of getting paying customers. One temple had over a thousand sex slaves working in the industry.

Christianity came along and said, in effect, that way of viewing sex is cheapening sex and uses people for selfish gain; there is something better. The desire you have is good and is part of our original design, but Christ has come and changed how to view your body. It has a meaningful design and purpose.

We have strangely adopted that view of sex in our pop culture around us. Most people today, including many in the evangelical church, view sex with anyone who is a willing partner as a normal way of life. One of the realities of being a new disciple of Jesus is that your body and how you use it sexually is not for you to decide. The only way we will see that though isn't through the rule against sex outside of marriage. It will happen when disciples of Jesus understand why they are using their bodies sexually outside of God's plan.

When you understand that what you are looking for — personal comfort of the experience or the approval of your lover or some sense of security in the relationship — is ultimately found in Jesus

Christ and all He has done for you. Only then you can turn away from seeking something besides Jesus and begin to live a life of love, not using people for your own selfishness.

Your personal life as it begins to align with God's way of life moves from a lifeless, fear-based conformity to an abstract rule to it being drawn to a God whose will for us is to make us whole and thrive in the way we were originally designed; "to glorify God by enjoying him forever" ("*Desiring God,*" John Piper).

The Missional Aspect

The third reality is the missional aspect of your life. "You are God's Temple..." (I Cor. 3: 16). What is a temple? People have built temples in all cultures, lands, continents, throughout generations (since the first people of Babel tried) to be places where they could connect to God, to fill the gap between man and whatever gods or beings were out there.

Temples have been places on earth where heaven intersects with us. It was a crossroad of the infinite and finite. In all the religious systems or religions that used temples, they were used as a place where people could connect to God. Cultures throughout history have used temples as a way to make life whole. As disciples we become the intersection of God and our neighbors. Why is a temple so important?

Think about Corinth. They had temples all around the city to their gods: Neptune/Poseidon or the sea god; Serapis, Isis were Egyptian gods; Zeus the Olympian god; Aphrodite and Venus, love gods.

Do you see how obvious this is? There's a gap. Every culture has acknowledged the gap and developed ways to relate to the gods; to the infinite. If we are ever going to get god to listen, to make peace, or make god happy somehow, we need a temple and need to make sacrifices. There are all kinds of false idols, gods; self-constructed ways to find wholeness. One might use money, sex, the sports channel, work, a child, a relationship, a house, some prestige or title, but something functions in life as the way to find peace.

John Smed is founder and president of Prayer Current. He writes, prays, and trains church leaders and church planting movement leaders to begin to pray like Jesus. He and I have been gospelling life together for over a decade.

In his book *"God in the Conversation,"* he tells of a time he grabbed a cab and engaged in a conversation with the driver. John jumped in, saying, "Do you mind me asking; are you Sikh?" "Yes, I am," the man replied. "So did you have a chance to say your prayers this morning?" Cheerfully he replies, "Yes, I said my prayers at six. I do so each day." "Did you go to temple?" John asked. "Oh, I go to temple each morning before work. I also go at the end of the day," he replied. "Prayer is at the heart of Sikh worship."

John answered, "Praying in a temple and praying anywhere is wonderful. May I tell you something even more amazing? This may surprise you...I do not have to go to temple to pray. I am a temple!" The cabbie was quite surprised and asked, "What do you mean?" John continued, "I believe God is in me and that I am in God. I am always in the place of prayer because I am always in the presence of God. The Bible tells us that if we believe in God's Son, Jesus, we become a temple" (2015, p. 7,8).

Ultimately, Jesus was the True Temple. He is the only one who closed the gap between us and God the Father. The ultimate Temple came down to us and became not just a place but the true sacrifice of Himself. The reason this is a reality of our Core Identity is from the gospel itself found in our Temple, Jesus. We don't go to the temple to make appeasement with God, to pray and gain his approval or make offerings to make some sort of deal with God. Christ is the temple, becoming the ultimate sacrifice needed to have God the Father's approval. "Therefore, since we have been justified through faith we have peace with God through our Lord Jesus Christ through whom we have gained access by faith into this grace in which we now stand. And we boast in the hope of the glory of God" (Romans 5:1-2).

God's Story is going somewhere. God has a mission and He has a people for his mission. If you go back to the Backstory of the Gospel Story (we will explore this in the next chapter), you find how the beautiful world God made was ruined and alienated. However God, in Christ, is going to reconcile ALL things, and He has given us a ministry of reconciliation. We are temples and were made for mission. Many disciples have lost the purpose or the passion to being the connecting place of the gospel to their neighborhood and have trivialized the Message to secondary things.

The Apostle Paul said, we manifest God to the world: "In Christ the whole building is joined together and rises to become a holy temple in the Lord and in Him you too are being built together to become a dwelling in which God lives by His Spirit" (Ephesians 2:21).

Peter adds, "...You like living stones are being built into a spiritual house... offering spiritual sacrifices... that you may declare the praise of Him who called you out of darkness into His wonderful light!" (I Peter 2:5).

Everyone here has a mission to be fully gospelling life together. We have to learn and listen to one another's stories as they relate to the Gospel Story and help one another connect the dots for those still in need of reconciliation with God. The great commission, "As you are going, make disciples of all nations..." is a major missional aspect of being a disciple of Jesus. Part of the call to being a Jesus' follower is to be about the business of His mission in making other followers of Jesus.

The Spiritual Aspect

The fourth and final reality is that Jesus Christ is your life. This is the spiritual aspect of the disciple's life. Once again the Apostle Paul reminded all the disciples living in the city of Colossae, a city in what is now Turkey, of a new reality of the Core Identity. His reminder is powerful: "Christ is our life" (Col. 3:4).

Everyone has a spiritual center because everyone is worshipping something. That is, everyone centers and orbits life around someone or something that gives them reason, meaning, or value. Before you became a disciple of Jesus your life was orbiting around something. Do you remember what it was?

It could have been a positive thing, like raising a family or being a good husband or wife, or getting a good education. It might even have been something very dutiful and religious. Or you might have lived life in self-damaging ways that brought great pain to you and others in your sphere of life.

In Biblical terms, those things are often termed idols. In religion they are known as the gods. Those gods make deals with you and promise blessings if you keep pursuing them, offering them worship in the highest place and promises of curses if you don't.

In *"Helping Others Change,"* Paul Tripp writes, "Scripture uses the term idolatry to describe a desire that rules my heart...What controls the heart will control the behavior. There is no situation or relationship where this battle is not taking place because we all tend to 'exchange worship and service of the Creator for worship and service of the created thing.'"

Worship is a delighting in and adoring of the One who made me, and though I had brought shame and guilt by disregarding Him and following my own ways and gods; nevertheless He gave Himself up for me. Not me giving myself up to Him so I can find acceptance. As one friend reminded me, "Jesus left the Most Affluent gated community in the universe and became poor so that you might become rich." If that doesn't grip your heart you're never going to worship Him. You will always look for something or someone to be your life.

In his book *"God's Passion for His Glory,"* John Piper writes: "Nothing makes God more supreme and more central in worship than when a people are utterly persuaded that nothing — not money, or prestige, or leisure, or family, or job, or health, or sports, or toys, or friends — nothing is going to bring satisfaction to their sinful, guilty, aching hearts besides God. This conviction breeds a people who go hard after God on Sunday morning. They are not confused about why they are in a worship service. They do not view songs and prayers and sermons as mere traditions or mere duties. They see them as a means of getting to God or God getting to them for more of his fullness — no matter how painful that may be for sinners in the short run."

If you have ever heard Tim Keller preach I suspect you have heard him say something along the lines of, "Christianity is a very practical faith. You can look at money and say, 'I'm glad I have you but you are not my life.' You can be glad to have a great career but say, 'You are not my life.' You can look at your husband or wife or kids and say 'I love you but at the end of the day, Christ is my life.'"

We have been called to enjoy life with God and others. That is the ultimate end of life. J.I. Packer summarized it well:

> "What were we made for? To Know God. What aim should we
> set ourselves in life? To know God. What is the eternal life
> that Jesus gives? Knowing God. What is the best thing in life,
> bringing more joy, delight, and contentment than anything
> else? Knowledge of God....Once you become aware that the
> main business that you are here for is to know God, most of
> life's problems fall into place of their own accord."
> ("Knowing God," 1975)

The four realities (outcomes or effects) of gaining a gospel understanding of your Core Disciple Identity will best be worked out with two or three other people with whom you are safely involved. Being listened to and understood by a couple of other people who you also listen to and understand is a powerful combination. When you allow yourself permission to "go it alone" or hide our true story in the safety of a large group you may feel stable and safe, but I suspect life is more sterile and fossilized than you care to let on.

Knowing and being known, the telling of one another's life stories, will allow you the opportunity to explore the motivational center of your being and begin the journey to life and freedom. To become what God planned for you to be before the creation of the world.

Dietrich Bonhoeffer, a German Lutheran pastor who was also a dissident of Hitler's Nazi regime, wrote a powerful book, *"Life Together."* Here is one insightful passage about the need of us being in a safe community:

> *"He who is alone with his sin is utterly alone. It may be that Christians, notwithstanding corporate worship, common prayer, and all their...service, may still be left to their loneliness. The final breakthrough to fellowship does not occur, because though they have fellowship with one another as believers and as devout people, they do not have fellowship as the undevout, as sinners. The pious fellowship permits no one to be a sinner. So everybody must conceal his sin from himself and the fellowship. We dare not be sinners. Many Christians are unthinkably horrified when a real sinner is suddenly discovered among them. So we remain alone with our sin, living lies and hypocrisy. The fact is we are sinners. But it is the grace of the Gospel, which is so hard for the pious to understand, that it confronts us with the truth and says: You are a sinner, a great desperate sinner; now come as the sinner that you are, to God who loves you...He does not want anything from you, a sacrifice, a work; He wants you alone. God has come to save the sinner."*

As you read, I trust you are seeing the joyful pursuit of being in gospel community as a saint/sinner who is serving both believers and not-yet believers in your sphere of influence.

Chapter Four

Gospelling Leads
To Change

"Well I got myself a T-shirt that says what I believe.
I got letters on my bracelet to serve as my ID.
I got the necklace and the keychain and almost everything
a good Christian needs, yeah.
I got the little Bible magnets on my refrigerator door.
And a welcome mat to bless you before you walk across my floor.
I got a Jesus bumper sticker and the outline of a fish stuck on my car.
And even though this stuff's all well and good, yeah,
I cannot help but ask myself--What about the change?
What about the difference?
What about the grace?
What about forgiveness?
What about a life that's showing I'm undergoing the change?
I'm undergoing the change.
Well I've got this way of thinking that comes so naturally.
Where I believe the whole world is revolving around me.
And I got this way of living that I have to die to every single day.
'Cause if God's Spirit lives inside of me, yeah...
I'm gonna live life differently"

"The Change," Steven Curtis Chapman

Have you ever stopped and asked yourself, "Why am I doing all this Christian stuff?" You go to church, read Christian books, listen to sermons, worship music or Christian music, but for what? If you have, perhaps your answer is because you really do want to be different. You honestly want to change and be a better person.

I have a pastor friend who told me that he doesn't believe people really do ever change. He believes that people are born with a certain DNA code to behave the way they do and you cannot change that. Really? Why would you spend all your life being the pastor of a church, preaching sermons and teaching Bible studies if you did not believe people will ever change? I would think I had wasted my life.

The man who mentored me years and years ago that the good news of grace was not just how you got into to God's family but also how you grow in God's family, has said more than once that he doesn't think he is going to get any better. I know he means it tongue-in-cheek because I have known him for over thirty years and he is different.

Personal change is not a minor issue. Jesus said, "If you do not change... you will not inherit the Kingdom of God" (Matthew 18:3). In other words, if you don't change you will not get God and that is a significant problem. We have been ruined and alienated from God and all things. We all know it. Our relationships are not the way they are supposed to be. We know we are not the way we were designed to live. I am not the man I ought to be. I am not the husband, father, grandfather, minister of gospel, president of a company, etc. that I ought to be or want to be. We know inherently that we need to change. We were made for more.

Our work in this world — even the world itself — is not functioning the way it was made. It has been separated from itself. In our spiritual center, we recognize our separation from God. There is a gap. Susan Ashton sang, "Sometimes I feel like there's a Grand Canyon between you and me," (Words Wayne Kirkpatrick 1996). To get reconciled we have to change. We know the sense of alienation all too often and might even say, "Something's gotta change if I'm going to make it."

Some people I know do not feel the need to change. They think of themselves as pretty good, moral, and helpful. They have a strong self-image and because they are not racists, murderers, or rapists there is not much need to change. And others feel so overwhelmed with their guilt or shame and feel they are so bad change is out of the question.

Is there hope for real significant life change? How do we move from simply restraining our more base selfish instincts to being men, women, teens or children who are experiencing a radically transformed life that is operating Relationally, Personally, Missionally, and Spiritually?

Everyone has a belief system of how they believe people change. You have a view in mind of how you can change yourself and it was probably taught to you in your childhood, somewhat adapted in your early teens, and morphed even more after your freshman year psychology class. The following are ways many people try to enact personal change in being a Christian or tell others how they can change.

You Need to Listen and Learn

Rarely taught overtly, but often taught by example, is the presupposition that people change by gaining enough of the right information. In too many churches we are told that we grow as we become learners of Jesus' teachings, doing what Jesus did, or joining Him in mission, etc. In this approach, change happens as we get more biblical information, more theology, and more homework. They might define discipleship as the process of transformation that changes us to be increasingly more like Christ but the way we are transformed is through getting the correct information and answers.

You Change Your Behavior

Another focus is on addressing the behavior; both restraining certain sins (rightly managing my sin) and being more diligent on reading the Bible, doing certain disciplines, and finding a place to serve at church. We have had scores of messages with examples of those who are faithful, hospitable, and obedient, and exhorted to follow their wonderful example. Similarly, we have heard messages or read materials that demonstrate the poor or sinful examples of people we are not to emulate.

Sermons and Bible studies are filled with exhortations to "Be like Peter" when he stood up for Jesus but not to be like him when he denied Jesus; "Be like Daniel" when he was so courageous; "Be like Paul" when he evangelized the lost. The false notion is that behavioral modification (rewarding good behavior and shaming bad behavior) will reinforce change.

Just Stop It

Many churches and sermons appeal directly to the will. Change happens as you choose what is right and the more right you do the more change will occur in your life; but you must apply your willpower. You may think I am exaggerating, but listen closely; have a notebook at hand and write down how many appeals you hear or read that are focused on building up your willpower. "Just stop it" is a recurring theme in many messages.

If moral conformity is what we are after then it makes sense to preach and teach to the will. "Don't look at ____, watch ____, drink ____ or smoke ____" Just fill in the blank. Just say no to sin.

Messages that appeal to the will are so commonplace that when you don't hear it you wonder if it was "Christian." I heard a famous USA pastor preach on the need for us to tell the truth. What was his motivational point as to why we need to tell the truth? "God told us to be truthful and you really don't want to be seen as liar, do you?" In shorthand, just stop it.

Surrender It All

Others suggest change happens through inspiration and experience. So, change occurs when we "surrender it all" to God and experience Him in a deeper way. The aim is to move to deeper and deeper expressions of emptying yourself of yourself. As you empty yourself of you, you add Christ and become like Him. This practice enjoys the weekly re-dedicating of my life to Christ at the close of Sunday services or listening to inspirational messages of lives that were changed through life experiences. It is found in the relentless singing of certain choruses, over and over, in heartfelt attempts to "fully surrender it all" and get more of God.

Until you are able to articulate how the gospel changes us you will be confused by diametrically opposed messages or be frustrated by inadvertently living as if knowledge or learning a certain set of skills or just being more dedicated and self-disciplined will change you. We will struggle to be free instead of being free to struggle in being made into the likeness of Jesus Christ, the Truest human.

How Do People Change?

Have you ever stopped and considered your own basic assumptions? Do not be too flip either with some catchy phrase — "Jesus is all we need" or "The gospel changes people." My question is, "How does Jesus change people?" or "How does the gospel change people?" Truth be told you are parenting, teaching a Sunday School class, spending hours counseling or caring for people with a belief in how they change. It really is a life and death issue. If we don't change, Jesus said, you don't get God.

I'm convinced that if the gospel of grace (that God in Christ has forgiven you of all your debt with Him and that He has freely given you all His "rightness") doesn't take your breath away something else will. And this world has lots of "something elses." I used to think that what God wanted for me to do was try harder, get more committed, deny myself, and keep my sin under control and then I would begin to see change. But the Christian life is the fight of faith to believe the gospel of grace really is true.

I Can't Dance

I grew up being taught that godly Christians don't dance. It was a sin and would lead to other sins. Somewhere along the road of righteousness I found grace really was grace, and law really was law...and grace won. Years later, when I became a pastor, people would ask, "Can Christians dance?" and I'd reply, "It is pretty obvious that some can and some can't. Just look at them on the floor." To be perfectly honest, I have the freedom to dance now, but I must admit even after lessons it's an ugly thing to watch.

Perhaps you grew up learning that the Christian life was a two-step: "Trust and obey, for there's no other way to be happy in Jesus but to trust and obey."

We were told to accept Christ as Savior for forgiveness, but then, at least in practice, we were driven to just try harder, obey more, do more, and resist temptation more. It was not in doctrine but practice: Accept Christ by faith and have your sins forgiven, but if you want to be blessed by God and be happy in your life you must try with all your might to obey the rules God has for you. I did the two-step for a long time.

Don't Dance, Hop

Later in my journey I met a group of Christians who said, "No way, baby. It is all of grace. Grace alone. There are no rules. The Christian life has got nothing to do with obedience and the second you say anything about obedience you are a legalist." It wasn't a two-step it was a one-hop.

It troubled me because I didn't see how grace was changing

anyone and I knew that the gospel of grace brings deep transformation in everyone who experiences it.

Michael Reeves, in his book, *"The Good God"* (in the US it is published under the title, *"Delighting in the Trinity: An Introduction to the Christian Faith"),* insightfully wrote:

"When Christians talk of God giving us 'grace' for example, we can quickly imagine that 'grace' is some kind of spiritual pocket-money he doles out. Even the old explanation that 'grace' is 'God's Riches At Christ's Expense' can make it sound like stuff God gives. But the word 'grace' is really just a shorthand way of speaking about the personal and loving kindness out of which, ultimately, God gives Himself...if [we] preach that God saves people by His grace alone, people will be given no reason to want holiness. After all if my holiness does not contribute in any way to my getting saved, why should I bother? I've got 'grace' after all...and that... fundamentally [misunderstands] salvation, as if it is something other than being brought to know, love and so want to please a beautifully holy God... Salvation is not about getting some thing called 'grace'—it's about freely receiving the Spirit, and so the Father and the Son."

A New Two-Step

Several years later another group came along and said, "Are you kidding me? The Christian life is by grace or believing but since you fail God all the time you have to repent every day." So, a new two-step was introduced to me: Faith in Jesus and personal repentance.

However, I watched many of them disrespect their wives and insult their friends or lose their temper at work and then simply say when confronted, "Yeah, I failed again and I have to repent." All they did was say "I believe in Jesus and I repent of my sin" again and again.

I didn't see any change. But isn't there something about having a new heart for following Christ in the idea of the gospel?

How Do We Change?

Remember Jesus said, "If you do not change you don't get God." So, how do we change? Do we change by the two-step? Is it Trust and Obey or Trust and Repent? Both seem to be very important. Or do we simply change by grace alone?

How you view this is vital to your own Christian life and gospelling life together. It really is at the heart of your belief as to how you change and how people change. If you think change happens by the growth of knowledge you will demand that we study, read, memorize, and gain more knowledge. If it is by willpower and determination, you will buckle down and make everyone else become more disciplined through rules and power. If it's through the emotional path of surrender, you will rely a lot on inspirational or shame based stories from the Bible, literature, or life experience. One of those techniques will be the operating system of your disciple-making approach with others.

Here is a key difference between religion and true Christianity: Gospel Christianity has at its starting point what religion has at its end goal. Religion is always looking for the way to GET right. All that a religious person does is in order to make themselves right. When all you have is religion, you try to fix yourself and your friends with rules, disciplines, guilt, or shame.

True Christianity is founded on the fact that we are already right with God and empowered by Him to a new life. All that a gospel Christian does is because he/she is right with God, perfectly.

The Gospel Dance

I want to suggest that the dance of the gospel is really a three-step, and the three steps that never stop. I list them as one, two, and three, but they are never-stopping and always in flow, like a beautiful dancer. As you read them you may wonder, "What about the place of prayer?" At the risk of offending those of you that have a "Prayer Changes Things" bumper sticker, I don't think prayer changes anything. However, the One we pray to does change things and He, as the first cause, has chosen to use our prayers as a second cause in the process of changing. But what do we pray to have Him bring change?

Let me suggest you pray these steps as you dance: "The Holy Spirit is the only One who can bring change. I cannot even change myself. But the Gospel is power and it can and will change anyone as the Spirit works" (Phil. 2:12,13).

Dance Step One: *Ongoing Repentance of Doubt and Disobedience*

Repentance is a humble expression of a desire for a renewed relationship with God — a relationship that we confess can be secured by His grace and mercy alone. We ask for pardon, presence, and His Spirit to reconcile us back from the damage we caused by our sin. This step, prayers of repentance, is missing in many modern music-driven churches today, both in corporate worship, and in small groups.

Professor of Practical Theology, Richard Lovelace noted,

"The root behind all other manifestations of sin is compulsive unbelief — our voluntary darkness concerning God, ourselves, His relationship to the fallen world and His redemptive purpose. For this reason the entrance and growth of new spiritual life involves the shattering of our sphere of darkness by repentant faith in redemptive truth" (*"Dynamics of Spiritual Renewal,"* 1995).

We pray to God, sometimes alone and sometimes with others, with sorrow for the personal approaches we take to "right" ourselves whether it's Relationally, Personally, or Spiritually. Our repentance goes deeper than simply the surface sins we regularly commit, to the things for which we are really living and striving; the things we consciously or subconsciously are doing to try and make our life "right."

We admit our own striving for wholeness through approval, comfort or security from others, from self-accomplishment, from this world's offers of life or even our religious successes, as if they are life.

Jerry Bridges, writer and scholar with *The Navigators*, wrote about how the gospel transforms us through the step of repentance:

"So repentance begins with an attitude of brokenness over our sin. But true repentance will be followed by an earnest desire and a sincere effort to put away the sin we are repenting of — to put on the Christlike virtues that we see missing in our lives. These efforts often seem to be characterized by failure as much as by success. But the frequent failures should bring us back to a broken and contrite heart that mourns over our sin. Brokenness, contrition, and repentance are all marks of a growing

Christian, a person who is experiencing the work of the Spirit in being transformed gradually more into the image of God's Son" ("The Transforming Power of the Gospel").

Prayers of repentance take center stage often in your C.R.O.S.S. community. We often fail in our relationships, intentionally and unintentionally hurting others around us. We break promises we've made to ourselves, to our spouses, our kids, our friends, and our colleagues.

We are all too often callous about being merciful to others in need, feel racially superior or missing our call to missional conversations with not-yet followers of Jesus. We lose faith. The famous rock band Fleetwood Mac told us we can "Go Our Own Way," and we have done so.

Yet all of those selfish choices can be joyfully brought back to Christ's power to rescue, renew, and restore through the choice of repentance. Community can be substantially healed.

Dance Step Two: *Ongoing Faith in Christ*

We believe and we continue to believe that we are made by God for His glory, that we are now forgiven perfectly by Jesus Christ through His death and resurrection and now as eternally loved adopted sons or daughters are fully made saints of God, able to say "Yes" to God with promised life with God. "The life *I now* live in the flesh (body) I live by faith in the Son of God, who loved me and gave himself for me" (Gal 2:20).

It is a fight of faith to believe God is truly good. Every day we realize we are accepted by God through Christ alone and not in anything we do. We rest in that. We realize He is always working for us as our advocate. We have a second Advocate, The Holy Spirit, alive in us that confirms and applies what the first Advocate has done on our behalf.

For me, I don't have a hard time believing the Gospel is true… for you. God loves you and accepts you and wants to do good to you. The problem is, I have such a hard time believing it's true for me. Luther nailed it when he said that we are born with an inborn suspicion that God is not for us. Like a bass note in a terrific song, I battle almost daily the constant thumping that because of my failures, sins, and selfishness I do not have God's favor. He seems to be never satisfied.

What is the answer? How do I keep on keepin' on? In a C.R.O.S.S community my friends remind me, like doubting Thomas after the resurrection, that Jesus Christ is alive now. The life, death, and resurrection of Jesus tells me that the lie is just that, a lie. God is satisfied because He was satisfied with Jesus; and I am in Him and He is in me. That's the antidote to the inborn suspicion — Faith that the Father is for me, because of the cross of Jesus. Daily it's a fight of faith; step one, to believe the Gospel is true. But I need a second step to admit my doubt and disobedience. However, there is a third step in the gospel dance.

Dance Step Three: *Our Generous Obedience to Christ*

Most of the writers of the New Testament filled their letters to the Christians with exhortations for them to love and obey God. They were never devoid of the realities of how God has changed them and that now they had a new affection to follow God but nevertheless each letter has continued calls to put to death things that destroy what we were meant to be and to put on the things that bring us into the renewal Jesus purchased.

In Paul's mini-bible, Romans, he clearly taught that we received grace to an obedience that comes from faith (Romans 1:5, 16:26). It is a call to what I refer to as "generous obedience" because it is not our way to earn what God in Christ as already done. Jesus' exhortation to love God and our neighbor is to lead us back to the place we were meant to be living a life of joy and gladness instead of hate, racism, slavery, poverty, rape, incest, addiction, or war.

> *"If you really want Jesus in the middle of your life, you have to obey Him unconditionally. You have to give up control of your life and drop your conditions. You have to give up the right to say, 'I will obey you if...I will do this if...' As soon as you say, 'I will obey you if,' that is not obedience. What that is really saying is: 'You are my consultant, not my Lord. I will be happy to take Your recommendations. And I might even do some of them.' No. If you want Jesus with you, you have to give up the right to self-determination"* ("Encounters With Jesus," Tim Keller).

We now have a new affection to obey Christ in worship, community and mission. Our freedom leads to generously follow God because we were made for good works that we would live in them. Jesus said it Himself, "If you love me, keep my commands" (John 14:15). When we love and generously follow his ways we are acting in freedom of what we were designed to be not acting or working against ourselves.

In 1547, John Calvin (the John Piper or Tim Keller of his day) wrote at the ripe age of 38, "I wish the reader to understand that as often as we mention faith alone in this question we are not thinking of a dead faith which worketh not by love but holding faith to be the only cause of justification (Galatians 5:6; Romans 3:22). *It is therefore faith alone which justifies and yet the faith which justifies is not alone:* just as it is the heat alone of the sun which warms the earth and yet in the sun it is not alone because it is constantly conjoined with light (*Antidote to the Council of Trent; emphasis mine*).

In a C.R.O.S.S. community, we help one another follow. We assist one another see the imago Dei and pursue life the way it was intended.

Will Is Not Enough

We might think that we can change our hearts by the sheer exercise of our wills, but haven't you lived long enough to discover that it will not last? All those promises, rededications, and New Year's resolutions just do not work. The truth is we are always controlled by our deepest passion; by what captivates our heart most.

Sam was working on his second church-planting project. He was married with a family and the work was going fairly well. One day over lunch he told me his sad story. He started playing on the web, surfing sites. Then, he met someone in a chat room.

The long and short of his saga was that he finally believed the lies being whispered into his ear... "You are not a good Christian nor a very good pastor; this isn't real. God is withholding something better from you; your wife is not enough... blah, blah, lie, lie, lie blah." One morning he got up and said, today's the day. He rented a U-Haul trailer packed his stuff then sat his wife and kids down and said, "I am leaving. I can't do this anymore." His wife was shocked, his kids devastated. He called the church leadership team as he pulled out of town.

Tears filled my eyes as he related his story to me. His sad tale has been told manifold times over. Sometimes it's the wife's story, but it's the same old blues.

What is the answer? Most of the messages I hear on this subject are more or less rules-based type exhortations: "Set up better accountability structures"; "don't look at pictures of naked people"; "put your computer in an open area."

Even the Proverb writer seems to warn us with the fear of loss and death when he wrote on the issue. But notice the writer's conclusion to all his warnings. "Do not let your heart turn to her ways or stray into her paths!" (Proverbs 7:25). Ah, the heart. The gospel in life aims for the heart.

Thomas Chalmers, a Scottish Presbyterian minister, preached a now-famously quoted sermon, "The Expulsive Power of a Greater Affection." Read some of what he said some 100 years ago:

"It is thus that the boy ceases at length to be a slave of his appetite, but it is because a more mature taste has brought it into subordination. The youth ceases to idolize sensual pleasure, but it is because the idol of wealth has gotten the ascendancy. Even the love of money can cease to have mastery over the heart because it is drawn into the whirl of [ideology] and now he is lorded over by a love of power. But there is not one of these transformations in which the heart is left without an object. Its desire for one particular object is conquered—but its desire to have some object is unconquerable. The object of the gospel is both to pacify the sinner's conscience and to purify the heart, and it is of importance to observe that what mars the one of these objects mars the other also. The best way of casting out an

impure affection is to admit a pure one...the only way to dispossess the heart of an old affection is by the expulsive power of a new one... it is only when admitted into the number of God's children through faith in Jesus Christ, that the spirit of adoption is poured out on us-- it is then that the heart...is delivered from the tyranny of its former desires" (Thomas Chalmers, 1830).

Sam concluded our lunch with the rest of his story. "After several months, I realized that I had been a miserable Christian, but I was a lousy pagan. I called my wife and asked her if I could come home and begin the work of restoration. She said "yes." Christ was the beauty his heart was really seeking, the comfort his soul longed for and the security to meet his broken masculine insecurity.

What we continue to have to teach ourselves is that, as Bryan Chapell writes, "Spiritual change is more a consequence of what our hearts love than of what our hands do. The spiritual disciplines are important but not as important as developing a heart for God. Hands and hearts coordinate and reinforce each other's functions in the biblical model of sanctification but the heart is the command center for every battle (*"Holiness by Grace,"* Bryan Chapell*).*

Summary

The Apostle Paul wrote in Titus 2:11-14 that the Gospel teaches us to say "No" to ungodliness (repentance) and worldly passions (strong over-desires) and to say "Yes" to live self-controlled and godly lives (obeying by a new and greater affection) because by faith we rely on Jesus Christ who gave His life to redeem us and become His very own! We live in repentance (putting off), following His will with ongoing faith in Him. The Gospel is news, but it is also power to transform all of us in need of change. British scholar and theologian, John Stott, concludes,

"We must put to death the deeds of the body or flesh, which is mortification. And we must set our mind on things of the Spirit, which is Aspiration. Mortification means a ruthless rejection of all practices we know to be wrong; a daily repentance, turning from all known sins of habit, practices, association or thought...The only attitude to adopt towards the flesh is to kill it. Aspiration (setting our minds on the things of the Spirit) is a wholehearted giving of ourselves, in thought and energy and ambition, to 'whatever is true and honorable, just and pure, lovely and gracious'. It will include a diligent use of the "means of grace", such as prayer, Bible reading, fellowship, worship, the Lord's Supper, and so on. All this is involved in setting our mind upon the things of the Spirit. Both mortification and aspiration are expressed by verbs in the present tense, because they are attitudes to be adopted and then constantly maintained" ("Men Made New").

Chapter Five

The Power of Gospel Story

*"A gentle breeze was blowing the air was
heavenly sweet- life was so complete.
In a picture perfect garden, while the sun went
down you could hear the sound
Of a man and woman crying, saying what have
we done?
We made a choice and now we're dying,
And we've got to leave this place and hide from
God's face.
But this is where we belong, you and I were
meant to be from now on.
Made by the Father, to live in His love, it's the
purpose and plan for the heart of man,
This is where we belong.
The warm winds of change were blowing after
years and years of hopeless tears.
One man became the doorway that would lead
back to the place where life was new.
A place just like the garden where we walk
and talk with God.
The way creation started, where each heart
and soul can come and be whole.
This is where we belong."*

"Where We Belong," Steven Curtis Chapman

We have seen so far that if we want to get God, who we as image bearers were ultimately to be in harmony with, we must be changed. We have seen that the Gospel of Christ is the only way we can have true change, one that transforms us into the original design — what we were meant to be — because His Gospel is power. We have also seen how change occurs in the application of the Gospel Dance: repentance, faith, and following. Would you agree that it is very important that we know what that Gospel is?

If you were going to explain the gospel to your neighbor or to a recent immigrant from a country where Christianity was unheard of where would you begin? How would you explain Christianity to another person? I suspect you would have to tell a story. Let me call it the Gospel Story. The gospel is more a story than it is a definition.

In 1977, moviegoers were introduced to a whole new universe through the magic storytelling of George Lucas. A galaxy run by a mystical and powerful "Force" that had both a good and bad side was in peril. As the soundtrack swelled audiences were invited into a story that was indeed cosmic in scope. We had no idea what to expect. How did Lucas, the creator, begin such a grand story? These now famous lines scrolled up the screen:

> "A long time ago, in a galaxy far, far away... It is a period of civil war. Rebel spaceships, striking from a hidden base, have won their first victory against the evil Galactic Empire. During the battle, Rebel spies managed to steal secret plans to the Empire's ultimate weapon, the Death Star, an armored space station with enough power to destroy an entire planet. Pursued by the Empire's sinister agents, Princess Leia races home aboard her starship, custodian of the stolen plans that can save her people and restore freedom to the galaxy..."

Those few words formed the back-story to the Star Wars film. It was brilliant. Without that short prologue we would not have understood the story we were about to be swept into. There would have been no understanding of the plot line, characters, or the struggle between the evil Galactic Empire and the well-intentioned Rebels. We were not told how the Empire came into being. We were not given information about all the planets, people, various alien beings, or the history of their galaxies. But we were given enough of the Backstory, the pre-history to put the whole movie into context.

Since the gospel is the power of God for salvation it is an imperative that we understand it. It not only has power, it IS power. It is an announcement of good news that has meaning and importance to your life here and now. We had better hear it and know it.

How Did We Get Here and Why Are We Here?

In our generation there are two prevailing backstories as to how we got here and why we are here. One storyline is that our universe is eternal; that is, there has always been something (matter, time and energy) and one moment in prehistory in a "Goldilocks condition... Bam, a Universe appeared" (David Christian, Ted Talk, www.ted.com *"History of the World in 18 Minutes"*).

That Backstory to our beginning, our "creation" if you will, has formed the West's cultural consensus during the past fifty years. If you are younger than 40 (especially 30 or under) you have been taught in every corner of culture from elementary school, high school, university, in music, movies, TV, art, business, friends, and pop culture that, "This is ONLY a Natural world. We live in a closed, mechanical and material world. There is no supra-natural. This is it. When you die, you die and you are food for the worms."

The explanation of our beginning is completely by naturalism: It is a Nothing-Nothing Backstory of our world and personal existence. It began by a cosmic accident and is therefore impersonal and only material. Men and women are finite. We are no different than any other animal or thing in the world or universe. We are just mechanically and chemically different. I do not mean to mock that belief system and we should be very careful not to do so with those who believe in the "god of nothing."

Richard Dawkins, the famous atheist who has made millions writing books against Christianity, admits in his book, *The God Delusion*, "I cannot know for certain but I think God is very improbable and I live my life on the assumption that he is not there" (pg. 51).

Although Dawkins and other believers in naturalism would never admit it, nevertheless, it is a faith system. The Naturalistic story is a faith story no matter if it's nothing-nothing or nothing-something.

Our whole existence according naturalism is that our thoughts, feelings, love, hate, passions, and desires are merely a result of our brain chemistry. Everything your mind tells you about the universe or God is just chemicals firing in the brain. Your whole existence is ultimately a collision chemicals bouncing around in the brain.

So, let me ask the obvious: if every thought is just a chemical reaction in the brain why is it true that we believe our thoughts are brain chemicals? That thought is simply a brain chemical reaction too. If we are purely physical and naturalistic, a combustion of exploding bodily fluids, we really have no reason, no basis to even believe our brains are made of chemicals.

Another problem with a naturalistic story is that it makes it impossible to find any meaning in this life, much less the universe. We have no ultimate reason. The cause for social justice, erasing racism, relieving poverty, or ending sex trafficking is only chemical explosions. There is no compelling reason for our existence. This is the dilemma of modern man. He is lost. He remains a zero. It is the damnation of our generation and the heart of man's problem. It has had an effect on you perhaps in ways you do not even know.

Any reasonable, thinking person would connect the dots from our culture's total absorption of the naturalistic view of life and the dramatic rise of depression, addictions, suicide, heroin overdoses, divorce, despair, and total disregard for life. The "god of nothing'" beginning is not good news. It is existential meaningless and is bad news for the human heart.

You have grown up with that belief system as the major bass note of life, sometimes subtly and other times not so subtly, pounding away at your heart. Maybe you had a university professor skeptically pound on your Supernatural approach to life, belittling or shaming anyone who held such "primitive views" of origin. Many are swept away and shipwrecked by those professors' faith in naturalism.

Do not let anyone buffalo you with the nonsense, "Oh you Christians just have faith, but I am more scientific than that." They have faith too. Their faith leads to despair and is not a compelling Backstory to our existence.

Knowing Gospel Story as the Framework for Gospelling Life

The gospel is more a story than a definition. In fact, the Bible is 70% story and those stories connect us to Gospel Story. The main Story is one of God's Rescue of His children and His runaway planet for the renewal and reconciliation of All Things (Col.1:19-20).

The rescue promised that a Hero would come (Gen. 3:15) and through the life, death, resurrection, ascension and return of God the Son, Jesus Christ, it was fulfilled. It is a compelling, cohesive, and true story as to why things are the way they are and why they are not as they "ought" to be. The four words to describe Gospel Story would be: Created. Ruined. Rescued. Renewed.

Gospel Story's Backstory opens with the simple words, *"In the Beginning, God created the heavens and the earth."* In fact, what the writer does in the first eleven chapters of Genesis is very simply answer basic questions that we would ask about any grand world-involved story. There is no expanded explanation.

The first question to answer is, "How did everything get here?" The answer: There is an infinite personal God who made it. God is the originator of everything. He made time and space. He maintains everything, moment by moment and controls the things He has made. Randomness and chaos are not reigning in this galaxy.

It is important to the Story that God spends only a few short verses in the whole Bible explaining how everything we see got here. He does not go into detail. This is only the Backstory to Gospel Story so it offers answers to basic first-things questions like: *"How did this galaxy get here?"* and *"Where did time and space come from?"* Many other words from God are written about his creative wonder later on. Here, in the beginning, it is short and basic. "Every house is built by someone, but God is the builder of everything (Hebrews 3:4).

The universe was made in a relational way, in that Earth is interconnected with all the other plants. Even our moon is related to the Earth. There is inter-relational connectedness in the ecosystems, animals, and atmosphere. It is quite complex.

God made all things beautiful and because He declared what he made "good," Earth and our solar system have moral value. That alone explains why we as creatures in the system can be awed by beauty of mountains, rivers and oceans, or by sunrises and sunsets.

The Earth and other created things have purpose and meaning. Fruit, minerals, water, seasons, vegetation were all made for a purpose of existence. And in a spiritual sense, all were made to glorify their Creator. The Psalmists frequently write about the mountains, trees, rivers and oceans crying out and glorifying God. King David wrote, "The heavens declare the glory of God; the skies proclaim the work of His hands (Psalm 91:1).

The Apostle Paul, when speaking at one of great cultural centers of world (like speaking at the Kennedy center in NYC), to the most elite class of leaders of their day, said, "The God who made the world and everything in it is the Lord of heaven and earth and does not live in temples built by hands. He himself gives all men life and breath and everything else. From one man He made every nation of men, that they should inhabit the whole earth; and He determined the times set for them and the exact place where they should live; God did this so that men would seek Him and perhaps reach out for Him and find Him, though He is not far from each one of us; for in Him we live and move and have our being" (Acts 17: 24-27).

He does the same thing in the philosophically pagan city of

Colossae by reminding the readers, "For by [Christ the invisible God] all things were created; things in heaven and on earth, visible and invisible... all things were created by Him and for Him" (Col. 1:15-16). Additionally, when Paul makes his case for the gospel in Romans 1, he explained God's anger against the world, by making the point of creation: "For since the creation of the world God's invisible qualities — his eternal power and divine nature — have been clearly seen, being understood from what has been made, so that men are without excuse" (Romans 1:20). Creation is vital to understanding Gospel Story's meaning.

When I was 10 years old, I went with a friend and his family to New Hampshire's White Mountains where we planted trees. A large field had been prepared for a tree farm in the middle of the forest. I don't remember what kind of trees we planted, but I do remember I was given a small piece of rope and told to stay on line and plant each little seedling at the end of my line. Now, years later, if a person were hiking through the randomness of the forest and expanse of the White Mountains and came across those trees perfectly lined up in exact distance from one another what would be a logical and reasonable conclusion? Someone intentionally planted these trees here. There is order and beauty here that is vastly different than the randomness elsewhere.

When we look at the universe we find order, beauty, and design. In God's Story, God does not argue origin. He doesn't bring any scientific explanation or defense. He simply says, "I am a Personal Father-Creator and I made it all." It is a simple, straightforward beginning written in an almost poetical fashion; *"In the beginning, God created the heavens and the earth."*

How Did We Get Here and Why?

Most people at some point in life ask themselves, "How did I get here and why am I here?" The legendary Beatle, George Harrison said in an interview on VH1 music channel, "It may sound like a lofty thing to say on VH-1, but basically what are we doing on this planet?"

The Backstory to the Gospel Story answers our questions. Again, it is Backstory that will be developed in the Story, but we need to know it to move ahead.

God is an eternal Father who has been in relationship with His eternal Son and eternal Spirit in perfect community. They have loved, communicated, and created. And by being so, They had no need for us, but we have need for Him. We love and long to be loved. We are made for relationship, companionship, and community. God said, "It is not good for man to be alone" and made a woman so they could be companions and multiply themselves, building a larger society of humans. There is male and there is female who are to be in perfect community with one another because that is the way God made us.

As personal beings we have beauty and dignity being made in His image. Unlike the other animals He made, we have a unique and valuable place in creation. We share the image of the Triune God who has been speaking before the beginning of our world. We too are verbalizers and communicators of ideas, interests, concepts, etc.

We know we exist as a "living being" and sense that we are made for something. We make choices and can share in emotion with others. We feel the wonder of a beautiful waterfall and have our breath taken away by the expansiveness of the galaxy or a snow-capped mountain range. We are moved by the beat of music or drawn into the power of a great novel. Man and woman were made physically beautiful. The strength of a man and the curves of a woman shout beauty and wonder.

Again, the Backstory does not get into a lengthy explanation to our human beginning, but Genesis does say that God made man and woman, *"imago dei"*, or in his image.

We were made with the mission to rule creation as God's vice managers, and to work and tend the garden. Adam's assignment to name the animals was given to him so he would understand and rule over them. Temporal in nature, our mission involves all the creation. Adam and Eve, our first parents, were made to find joy in God; placed in the Garden of Eden to rule it, work it and to love each other as one flesh. Ultimately, we were made to connect completely in all of our being, including spiritually, with God; to connect and remain connected to the source of all that is good and all that is life.

This is a God unlike any other god in history, religion, or mythology. He does not need anything from us. We do not fill a void or provide service to Him as if he needed love or adoration. He is absolutely sovereign, infinite, all-sufficient, self-existing, self-sustaining, glorious, all-knowing, all-wise, all-satisfying, always present, merciful, gracious, and abundantly good.

Even after decades of teaching that there is no God and that humans are only here through a natural evolutionary process of time plus chance, the majority of people living in the world today and throughout the history of the world have accepted and believed in some type of Supra-Natural Maker or Creator. Gospel Story begins with good news. We were made to enjoy God's presence and glory. He is the best thing in the universe. What an amazing beginning to this grand Story! It really is good news.

Why Things are Ruined and Not the Way They Ought to Be

The Backstory also reveals the tension and it is vital to know this in order to understand the rest of Gospel Story and your story. Adam and Eve were living a full and meaningful life in a perfect Eden. The evil one tempted their hearts, "Doubt God and trust yourself." He wickedly asked, "Did God really say?" He tempted them with unbelief. He tempted them to live life autonomously. Author John Eldredge reminds us,

> *"Every story has a villain... though most of you do not live like it. Most people do not live as though the Story has a Villain, and that makes life very confusing. How have we missed this? All the stories we've been telling about the presence of an evil in the world, all the dark characters that have sent chills down our spines and given us restless nights—they are spoken to us as warnings. There is evil around us. War. Famine. Betrayal. Murder. Surely we know there is an evil force in this world."*

Our first parents were lured by the promise of complete freedom from God; to live as their own "gods," free to choose their own way, with boundless and limitless opportunities currently unknown to them. They did not want to be image bearers of God, they wanted to be a god. Instead of trusting God and his promise of life they believed the lie, willingly rebelled, and ate from the Tree they had been told specifically not to..

Significant emphasis is placed on this one event because it frames the rest of Gospel Story. Not only is there good news but also there is bad news. This single historical event answers two more main questions most of us even in all our various cultures have asked: "Why is this place such a mess and why am I such a mess?"

Gospel Story offers a unique insight into the reason why you can't always do what you know you should do.

If you missed the reality of the tragic scene with Adam and Eve doubting and disobeying God it would be like missing the fact that there is an evil Galactic Empire bent on destroying the planets before watching Han Solo and Luke Skywalker shoot it down to rescue Princess Leia.

In Gospel Story, we discover there is personal evil in the universe, a Darth Vader if you will. The Evil one came and tempted Eve to doubt God's love and goodness. And man chose to believe in themselves rather than the God who had made them and given them life.

The first Adam, along with Eve "vandalized God's shalom" as Cornelius Plantinga, Jr. said in *"Not the Way Its Supposed to Be: A Breviary of Sin,"* and immediately their harmonious and beautiful world began to disintegrate. Alienation occurred in Adam and Eve's relationship. Blame shifting began at once: "The man said, 'The woman you put here with me — she gave me some fruit from the tree and I ate it.' Then the LORD God said to the woman, 'What is this you have done?' The woman said, 'The serpent deceived me, and I ate.'"

I'm not very good at marriage counseling, but I can easily imagine what the relational temperature was like in their home that night. Adam blamed Eve and God for his failure and she blamed the devil. This explains why we are alienated in our human relationships. Our marriages are not the way we want them nor are our relationships with our kids, neighbors, other races, or nations. Gospel Story explains the seeds for racism, injustice between people and other relational or sociological crimes and decay. A long, long time ago, in a garden far, far away....Adam was alienated from himself and Eve from herself. "They realized they were naked" and tried to cover themselves and hide. They felt true moral shame for the first time in their lives. Prior to their rebellion "they were both naked and felt no shame" (Gen. 2:25). Their inner souls felt legitimate guilt and anguish for their rebellion. They felt alone in the universe.

You are not the person you want to be and you know it. I hide and you hide. Personal alienation explains a lot of our inner brokenness and sense of aloneness. It can also explain illness, cancer, mental breaks, and physical handicaps. It explains why my daughter, along with hundreds of thousands of other kids, was born with genetic brokenness and disability, why your mother suffered from a brain tumor, and why your friend's son has autism.

The Backstory explains the addictions we have and the surgeries we need. We are dying too young. We now understand why we feel naked, vulnerable, and alone because the Backstory has given us a context. It makes sense. It is unfair and not right but at least we can understand why. The ruin and alienation we have endured were not part of the original design. We know that God is not a moral monster by creating such a messed up world. Our first dad and mom did it to us.

Humanity was alienated from the mission that God had created them for. The mission to rule the earth and animal kingdom had been ruined. Instead of ruling as God's managers they struggled with created things. Sin unleashed its cruelty and harshness on the natural world. God said there will be thorns and thistles and meaning from work will now be ruined as it becomes hard and unrewarding. There will be ecological consequences from the rebellion because all creation was ruined. Many today who say man is responsible for our ecological problems have no idea they are agreeing with Gospel Story.

Ultimately, the most damaging separation was their relationship with God. God promised death if Adam and Eve did not obey his one thing. They did not believe him. The loving God judged their sin and fulfilled His promise that the day they disobeyed they would die. Spiritual death came. By their own action Adam and Eve were now on the road to death — physically, spiritually, and eternally — and so are you. The chances of you dying are one out of one. This is bad news.

One Sunday, a little boy showed his parents his drawing from his children's church class at lunch. His dad asked, "So what is this?" The boy said, "This is a garden called Eden." The dad pointed to what looked to be a car with one person driving and two people in the back seat and asked, "What is this then?" "Oh," said his son, "That is God driving Adam and Eve out of Eden."

When you miss the point of tension, of ruin and alienation, of curse and death, the rest of the Gospel Story does not make sense. If you miss the crushing blow to the entire cosmos God made — you can work, write, ignore, or explain it all away — but you will struggle the rest of your story trying to make sense of your life. After Adam and Eve's decision they are cursed and thrust out of Eden.

Gospel Story's Backstory explains this and it explains why you are alienated from God and under the death curse. No one is right, not even one. All around the world, through all times in history and nations, humans have known there is a gap between them and God. We need a Story that makes sense of why "We long for the shape of things to be true to their form 'Benediction'"(lyrics by Wayne Kirkpatrick and Billy Simon, 1991).

A friend's voice mail introduction says, "It's a hostile world so we have to stick together. Leave me a message and I will get right back to you." This world is brutal at times. We feel the ruin and alienation. When we experience a sense of fullness, beauty, or security, we think, "This is where I belong." We want to know God and know we are loved and accepted. We want our own "Eden" to enjoy with our loved ones. But when tragedy hits or injustice occurs we instinctively cry out, "This isn't right and there must be another day coming." Where did that get into our souls? Not from an impersonal, natural cosmic accident of atoms and energy.

Gospel Story offers a compelling rationale for why the world is both wonderful and hostile at the same time. It also explains how humankind can be both beautiful and cruel at the same time. It explains why we feel alienated from our world, our work, others... even ourselves. It helps give context to feeling all alone in the universe.

The Backstory covers two main points of The Story, namely, Creation and Ruin (or Alienation). It is clear from the moment of our first parents' decision that there was going to be a need for someone to reverse the direction of the runaway creation and rescue us. We certainly were not going to rescue ourselves from our self-made ruin. You can't be the hero of your story and rescue yourself even though you may try. All along the way the Story has dropped hints about the main character of the Gospel Story — The Story's True Hero. God gives hope that although we are left in this crazy place this craziness isn't the end.

Rescue

Gospel Story is the rescue and renewal plan. God through the Hero of the Story, His Son Jesus, is the One who will come, and now we know, has come to rescue His runaway planet. "For He has rescued us from the dominion of darkness and brought us into the kingdom of the Son He loves, in whom we have redemption, the forgiveness of sins" (Col. 1:13, 14).

There was a need for a second Adam to rescue us because the first one messed it all up. "Death came through a man, the resurrection of the dead comes also through a man... for as in Adam all die, so in Christ all will be made alive" (I Cor.15:21, 22 and Romans 5:17-21). Jesus, as the second Adam, became the "true Undercover Boss."

He came not to help us become better people, but to transform us in a fundamentally unique and compelling way into something different than we were.

Jesus Christ did that by being ruined on our behalf. He was alienated from God the Father in the ultimate alienation for our guilt and moral shame, taking our rightful judgment. When He stood silent before Pilate and offered no defense for the charges against Him, it wasn't because He didn't have one, for He was innocent. But He was at that moment representing you and there was no defense to be made.

And His death and resurrection became your death and resurrection. It was the death of death, and Life was granted. Eternal, glorious and joy-filled life, and everyone who believes (not achieves) God's rescuer has that life. "Whoever has the Son has life. Whoever does not have the Son does not have life" (I John 5:12).

Gospel Story confirms our innate sense that we need to be

rescued but know we cannot rescue ourselves. Someone has to come from the outside. This world may have told you that all you need is inside your own self, look within; if you believe it you can achieve it. But you know, you know, it simply is not true. All the beauty I need is not in me. But the Good News is we have been rescued.

Renewal Of All Things

The Apostle Paul continued in Colossians to declare, "and through Him (Christ) to reconcile all things to Himself, having made peace through the blood of His cross; through Him, *I say,* whether things on earth or things in heaven. And although you were formerly alienated and hostile in mind, *engaged* in evil deeds, yet he has now reconciled you in His fleshly body through death, in order to present you before Him holy and blameless and beyond reproach" (Col 1:19,20, emphasis mine).

"Christ has died. Christ is risen. Christ will come again." is an acclamation used in thousands of churches throughout history. Jesus Christ promised, "I will come again" and historic, orthodox Christians believe despite over two thousands years after his promise it is true. When he returns he will bring judgment on those who have hated him and will also renew us and the earth.

Paul informs us that the enemies of the gospel have as their destiny destruction but that "...our citizenship is in heaven. And we eagerly await a Savior from there, the Lord Jesus Christ, who, by the power that enables Him to bring everything under his control will transform our lowly bodies so that they will be like his glorious body" (Phil. 3:20-21).

He will recreate the old and bring the new, including you and me. "Then I saw a new heaven and a new earth...I saw the ...new Jerusalem, coming down out of heaven from God... And I heard a loud voice from the throne saying, 'Look! God's dwelling place is not among the people, and he will dwell with them" (Rev. 21:1-3). The model of a gospel-saturated Christian is a return to the original, but uniquely glorified human experiences of how we were meant to be. And so will this earth, which now groans in her ruin.

Conclusion

So, what does Gospel Story have to do with "Gospelling Life Together?" Practically everything. It is the foundation of our relationship to God and one another. As you and I explore Gospel Story together, we discover the wonder of God, His power, His holiness, His plans, His work, His love, His beauty and glory. By the Story we find rescue and understanding for our lives as well as the world He made. Singer/songwriter Randy Stonehill sang, "I don't want my life to end not ever knowing why it began" ("*First Prayer*").

Every time I teach through Gospel Story to a group of coach trainees or in another retreat forum I am amazed and humbled at the enormous effort and cost to reconcile me back to God, my Maker. The Gospel Story isn't about what you have to do to get God, it is what God has done to get you. Gospel Story is about God and what He has done and is doing to renew or re-create what His rebellious and arrogant creatures ruined; our relationships with others; our relationship with ourselves; our relationship with the mission God had for us to rule His creation; and our relationship with God Himself.

A friend, who is at the very least a self-proclaimed atheist and at best an agnostic, once told me, "The problem with what you believe Tom is this: It is *just (emphasis his)* a story. It is a fable, and stories and fables don't change anything." Indeed, it is a Story, but it is a historically accurate, compelling, cohesive, and True Story. It is a revelation from the God who made us, to us.

To paraphrase the Westminster Divines, (They are not a band, but a council of theologians which met to restructure the Church of England from 1643-1653). Gospel Story is majestic in its style. From beginning to end it has one main theme, to declare the excellence and beauty of God's glory to the whole earth by showing his graciousness and love in redeeming and reconciling to himself a people and renewing all things. All the years of work by its critics to destroy its reliability have not dented its power one whit.

Yet with all that I must admit that I cannot prove to my agnostic friend that Gospel Story is true. The Holy Spirit of God Himself must do that. However, I did respond to him, "If this world is only a material, natural world then the accumulation of material things — money, status, houses, cars or political power — would provide you meaning. Yet, I know you know your natural story is not providing you meaning. You know there is more to this life."

Chapter Five

Chapter Six

Telling Our Stories To One Another

"They say there is a story being told
Bigger than I can comprehend.
And in the rumors I can hear an invitation calling.
This is the, the big story.
There is a God who's in control.
Telling the, the big story.
And He wants us to know we will find ourselves
when we lose ourselves
in the bigger story.
Come and take your place in the story."

"The Big Story," Steven Curtis Chapman

Emily Phillips, a 69 year-old Florida grandmother, was diagnosed with cancer and given a short time to live. She penned her own obituary and asked her daughter to post it on Facebook after her death.

This was her posthumous entry: "It pains me to admit it, but apparently I have passed away. Everyone told me it would happen one day, but that's simply not something I wanted to hear, much less experience. So, I was born, I blinked and it was over."

Someone said to me once, "I can describe my life story in four words: Born. Work. Accumulate. Die." I shared that with friends in Cuba and one said, "For me it would be: Born. Work. Survive. Die." What four words would you use to define the story of your life? How is your life story compelling and cohesive?

You may have already noticed that your story follows the same pattern of Gospel Story. There is a Backstory that begins with good news, explains the bad news, so that we can have really Good News. God is on mission to rescue and renew you and all things through the life, death, resurrection, ascension, and return of His Son, Jesus.

We will never know our own story or make any sense of our lives unless we know the Gospel Story. Knowing about God without knowing self can lead to pride. Knowing self without knowing God could lead to despair. In order to really know yourself you have to get outside yourself. That is what a love-filled community of others can do. They help interpret your story in light of Gospel Story.

"Our life is a story. A rather long and complicated story that has unfolded over time. There are many scenes, large and small and many 'firsts'. Your first step; your first word; your first day at school. There was your first best friend; your first recital; your first date; your first love; your first kiss; your

first heartbreak. If you stop and think about it, your heart
has lived through quite a story thus far"
("Waking the Dead," John Eldredge)

It is why you and the others you've invited into C.R.O.S.S. community should spend a lot of time on the Gospel Story, making sure you get THE main point. In C.R.O.S.S. community we explore the how and why the Father made you; how the fall has ruined, alienated you and cursed your world and your created design; how Christ rescued you and is reconciling you to God; and what mission the Spirit intends for you to be a part in the renewal of all things. If you want to end up living a miserable life, live as if you are the hero of your own story and doing your own thing. Freedom will come as you see Jesus as the true hero of your story.

"Discipleship — following Christ — means being called away from our dead-end plots to become part of His story; to be taught by Him so that we find ourselves entrusting our lives to Him in growing confidence. Only then can discipleship be something other than a lot of busywork" (*"The Gospel-Driven Life,* "Michael Horton).

Carla lived the only kind of life that she knew. Growing up, her parents were mostly absent and she never really heard about God. All through school she was taught naturalistic evolution and so her life was only in and of this world. As a young adult woman she was her own master. For her that meant following her desires which led her to work hard and put in long hours in order to have a successful career, but when the weekends came she partied hard with her few friends.

She was very driven and highly successful in her career yet no one knew that she battled inner self-doubt and often struggled with patterns of despair and despondency. Her therapist told her that her problem was she looking for her self-worth in her career and might consider looking for a relationship instead.

When a friend at work invited her to visit her church, Carla, a self-proclaimed agnostic, wanted to be open minded and thought maybe she would find something good at a moral place like church. On her first visit the people she met seemed normal, caring, and fun. She attended a home group a few weeks later and discovered the men and women really cared deeply for one another, could laugh and have a great time without having to get drunk to do it. She had never seen people care the way they did and wanted to know more.

Her friend, Lisa (who had invited her to church) and Sue (one of the women from the group), asked if she would be interested in getting together one afternoon. Carla was glad for the interest and soon the three women were meeting every Thursday afternoon. Carla did not know it when she said "yes," but she had joined a discipleship group.

Inside of four months, Lisa and Sue celebrated with Carla her new birth in Christ. Later, when Carla told her pastor about her journey, she said she was out one weekend with her regular crowd of friends who were partying and "All of sudden I had this sense, this pressing reality, that this was not my life. I had found a new life."

She continued, "No one had told me I couldn't go out and party or that it was wrong. In fact, Lisa and Sue told me I should keep hanging out with my friends. But I knew, I just knew that I was different. There was a God who had loved me and Jesus had died to give me life and make me whole. I had changed."

As we are Gospelling Life Together using Gospel Story with Jesus at the center we will be kept free from becoming pragmatic moralists or self-congratulating dogmatists. If we see Gospel Story as primarily a life guide or the Bible as a moral book of virtues our lives will whither and die or become mean and militant, using Christianity as a weapon.

Gospel Story is a love story. It's a Story of how God loves his children and creation, and comes to rescue them from their alienation, slavery, nakedness, lost-ness, darkness, blindness, death, enemy status, cursed, exiled, and orphaned lives, so as to renew, free, adopt, clothe, find, heal, befriend, and make whole so they flourish into what He had originally made them to be; humans in the image of God.

Your Life has a Backstory

As we have seen, you were made by an all-glorious, all-good, all-holy, and all-loving God to be in relationship with Him and with others so that He might display His glory in all of His creation because He is the greatest good in the universe. You were made with excellence, beauty, and worth. You were created for a purpose and meaning in this world. You have a mission, a certain gifting, with strengths, artistic talents or abilities and passions to do things you both enjoy and provide a sense of dignity.

When you accomplish those things that have you say, "This is what I was made for," you are in some small way connecting to the mission God has for you. There is a compelling reason why you exist and why you will continue to exist. You are way more than a mush of chemicals swishing around in your body. It is Good News.

Telling Your Story: Beginning

Someone once said, "The two most important days of your life are the day you were born and the day you figured out why." To understand the second day, it's important we look back to where and when we were born. Oftentimes we just jump right in a group with where we are now, what we do for a living, and what neighborhood we live in. We throw in our past church experience and some other work-related trivia. We share our kids' names, ages, schools as well as our favorite sports team or alma mater. Rarely do we go back to the beginning. It is here we can discover our story has a good news beginning.

Consider how you were made and placed in a certain family of relationships. Your parents are unique to you. I see my parents differently than my brothers and younger sister. They had interactions and bonding times that were different than mine.

Your birth order and how you related growing up with your siblings has had a great deal of influence on you. Did you grow up around aunts, uncles, and cousins or did you only see them on holidays? For some, it was a grandparent who had significant influence in their lives. I want that to be true for my grandchildren.

You grew up in a certain neighborhood with a unique culture. The fact that you were born and raised in the city of Boston or Miami instead of rural Georgia or Alabama is part of your unique story. The kids you had as friends in various schools growing up are all part of how you became you. Teachers and coaches informed your self-view. They formed you in the early years like friends formed you in your teen years. All of that matters in you knowing you. It was not an accident nor a random thing, "floating around like a feather."

You were made as image bearer of God. How is that unique to you? You have certain skills and interests. Can you think about times in your Backstory that shaped those interests or allowed you to develop in some skill area?

Each of us has a knowledge base and some are better than others. Now we know because of genetics that each of us has a unique set of DNA. The interest today to sign up and have an ancestry check done is at some level a desire to know ourselves, our past, and our stories. You have seen the TV commercials that reveal how the person thought they were of one heritage only to learn they were a mix of several. We are each unique.

You were also made to contribute in some way to your world and the lives of others in a meaningful way through work. Your work matters to God. Some of you have certain talents in business and know how to start companies, make money or put people to work. I am always fascinated to talk with business leaders who have amazing talents to create a company. For others it is science, or design, art or engineering.

My three daughters grew up with their own unique sense of mission in their lives. Do you have awareness of the mission God was preparing for you? What people in your life told you, "You are really good at that?"

They were pointing out your created missional purpose. As a disciple of Jesus, part of our missional design is to intentionally remain witnesses to the resurrected, living Christ.

A friend of mine told me he did not become a God follower until his mid-twenties, but said he was always interested in God and spirituality even as a young boy. Why was that? The desire to connect with the spiritual world spans generations, history, and cultures. It is what the African monk, St. Augustine, meant when he wrote, "You have made us for yourself and our hearts are restless till they find their rest in you."

How old were you when you first sensed that there was something or someone greater than you could dream?

As a young emerging pastor, one of my favorite writers was Gordon MacDonald. In his book, *The Life God Blesses,* he retells a story of a man in his disciple community who told about an event in his growing up years. It had an enormous impact on my life and thinking. Let me allow his pen to encourage you:

> "My grandfather was a farmer and he had all the regular kinds of farm machinery — trucks, tractors, that sort of thing — and he taught me how to drive each of them in the summer. Well there was this one day — I was about 12 — when he and I were out in the field and he said to me, 'Run back to the barn and bring the truck out here'. I was thrilled that he'd asked and I went to the barn, got into the truck and started to back it out. But I turned the wheels too quickly and suddenly I had the front bumper of the truck wedged into the side of the door. And it seemed if I went forward or backward I was going to hurt either the truck or the barn. I was devastated because I figured that Granddad would see that I wasn't old enough to be driving his machinery. But I had no choice in the matter so I went back out to the field and said, 'Granddad, you've got to come and help me. The truck's stuck in the doorway.' He stood there for a moment quietly looking at me, stroking his short beard. And then he said, 'Son it seems to me that if you got the thing stuck you can go back and get it unstuck.' I never loved my grandfather more than I did at that moment. Now my father would have said something like, 'Can't I ever trust you to do a thing right?' Or 'How many times do I have to tell you how to do something? Come on I'll do it

myself.' Not my grandfather. He knew something about how important it was for a boy to keep his dignity even if it meant a little crinkle in the fender of a farm truck."

For about the first decade of my Christian journey I thought God was like the dad in that story. I'd fail at His command and He'd be so ticked. Now I know He's not. I still fail. But I know that He's not ticked. It formulated part of my story and spiritual identity.

Telling Your Story: Ruin

All our stories include the reality ruin or alienation. No life this side of Eden is exempt. We can remember those times when we knew we lived in a broken down place. For some it still brings such a deep sense of loss and shame that they do not want to allow themselves to "go there" anymore. For others the ruin is so powerful they tattooed it on their bodies. Every time I teach on this, someone will begin to tear up because we live with our story.

As we talk about our stories and begin to open up one of the key places where we experienced alienation was in a relationship. Maybe it was the loss of a parent through divorce or death. Another, it was the life-changing event of abuse. Loss, betrayal, anger, and conflict, all make us well aware that our relationships are not the way they were meant to be.

In a powerful scene from the blockbuster movie *"Forrest Gump,"* Jenny, Forrest's love since childhood, has come back to Greenbow, Alabama, after being on the run for many years. They are out walking one day and came across the now vacant and dilapidated house where Jenny had grown up and been abused by her father. She slowly walked barefoot toward the run-down shack and all of sudden threw her shoes at it.

She then picked up rocks. In a fit of rage she began to throw the rocks at the house yelling, "How could you do that to me?" She finally stopped and collapsed onto the dirt road, weeping. Forrest made his way to her and sat down in the dirt next to her and in the off camera commentary said, "Sometimes I guess there just aren't enough rocks."

There aren't enough rocks to deal with the wounds of this world. There will never be enough rocks to throw at the pain people have or will bring into your life. There will be people in your past you will have to forgive.

My wife, Rachel, is an incredible woman with whom these past decades together I have learned daily gospel living. Every day we share with one another how God is working, leading, speaking, teaching, and changing us. She has the gift of prayer and intercession, along with hospitality. She journals every day and allowed me to read this entry a few years ago:

> "In the heart of God is love and relationship. That's how God thinks and works. God is more interested in relating than with a program of action. When God acts it is for the sake of relationships. When Jesus was here He showed us His mission was people, not a system of rules. He approached people with love, forgiveness and acceptance, the very heart of God. What angered Jesus the most was when a system replaced relationship. He came to show people the way to repair their broken relationships with their Creator. Jesus' purpose was to rebuild our relationship with Him by suffering the ultimate relational divorce — separation from God. Eternal death is our soul completely separated from a loving God. Sin brought the darkest aloneness and separation from the loving heart of God. Our enemy and God's enemy will make every possible attack on relationships. He seeks to destroy human

relationships that cause rippling effects on our relationship with God. The enemy will mess up our view of a loving relational God by cheating you of a childhood relationship that should have been safe, but was not. Or by taking away a bonding with another person that should have been loving and nurturing. If Satan can rob us and confuse our view of God, he can keep a personal loving God as a foreign concept. But God alone can restore our souls with a whole view of relationship. God can take the broken, damaged view, and restore it with Himself."

We know all too well our own sense of personal ruin. Even at a young age our sense that we are not "ok" is pressing. When I was in high school (no, it wasn't a one room school house!), I remember a teacher asking us to write down 10 things that if we could we would change about ourselves. Most of us felt limited by only 10.

We were teens who hated our curly or straight hair. Different noses, chins, fewer pimples, less thighs or skinny legs; all were listed. Yet had we'd been honest, there were character qualities we lacked, in which we felt shame or ruin.

No one is immune from a sense of shame, guilt, or weakness. We might have personal challenges with physical or mental health issues, such as depression. Personal ruin includes those times in our Backstory where we felt unworthy or enslaved to our passions or all alone in the universe. We are not "ok" and no matter how much your parents, teachers, or society tried to tell you that you are basically good and a winner you knew you were not.

As we continue in community we can find the sense of ruin in the way God made us to work. God put us here with ultimate meaning, but also temporal purpose to be stewards of the creation He made. However, as we saw, it has been ruined. We know it. Somewhere in our Backstory our spiritual centers get strangled out. Sometimes the line between living for self and finding life with God can be remarkably thin. Our stories are filled with broken, ragged edges of life and ruin and we have been bloodied up by it all. In fact, we are spiritually dead in our sins and shame.

You may have thought even then you were your own man or woman. Like William Henley in his famous poem, Invictus, you said, "I am the master of my fate; I am the captain of my soul." However, you were born under a curse and are a slave to this world and to desires that worked against you. In one sense you have never been your own and in another you have been only your own. This is the bad news of our own story. You cannot change your Backstory, but you can change, or better yet, God can change the future where that old Backstory was taking you. Life is not fixed.

Telling Your Story: Rescue

If you are reading this book I assume you became a disciple of Jesus at some point in life. That is the aim of Gospel Story, that Jesus came to rescue us from the dominion of darkness and brought you into His very own Kingdom of life. What a remarkable thing that is when you think about it. It really is very good news!

Years ago, and maybe in some tribes they still do, we used to call it giving your testimony. When I was a teen, most testimonies were about how sinful a life the person had lived, offering details of sinful behaviors and then a quick summary of them "accepting Jesus as my Savior" and now "I am saved and not going to hell." The prodigal son came home. I was always more fascinated with the stories of crime, drugs, and moral failure rather than the rescue.

If you are a disciple of Jesus then you do have a story of rescue. It might have been dramatic or maybe you really don't remember a time when you didn't know Jesus rescued you. But you have been rescued and that is the major turning point of your story. The price Jesus paid to redeem and rescue should overwhelm even the best of us.

The Apostle Paul was one of the most rule-following religious zealots that walked the planet. He had been raised in the law. He grew up following it. He was the type of person who would never have "smoked, chewed or hung around with the girls that do." Even from childhood he did what the law of God demanded, at least outwardly. At one point he even wanted to kill anyone who in his view blasphemed the name of God.

Later in life he wrote about his rescue from his damnable good works: "Whatever was to my profit (all the rule keeping one could muster) I now consider loss for the sake of Christ... that I may gain Christ and be found in Him not having a righteousness of my own that comes from the law but that which is through faith in Christ — the righteousness that comes from God"(Phil. 3:7-9).

In another place he confessed, "Even though I was once a blasphemer and a persecutor and a violent man I was shown mercy because I acted in ignorance and unbelief. The grace of our Lord was poured out on me abundantly. Christ Jesus came into the world to save sinners — of whom I am the worst. But for that very reason I was shown mercy so that in me, the worst of sinners, Christ might display His unlimited patience" (I Tim. 1:13-16).

Oftentimes small groups, home churches and even personal discipleship pairings focus primarily on the subject or book they are studying with no appreciation or context from where each person has come. It is hindering the effectiveness, especially among the new generation, in bringing them along to maturity. To be transformed into the image of the True Man, Jesus Christ (or to be made into what we were originally designed by our Maker to be) will be helped by thinking and reflecting on our good news, bad news, and very good news. And we can find that best in community while others we love, help interpret our good news and bad news.

Telling Your Story: The Renewal of All Things

God is going to renew all things and you are part of that renewal. Paul affirmed in Colossians 1:19,20, "For God was pleased to have all His fullness dwell in Him and through Him to reconcile to Himself all things, whether things on earth or things in heaven, by making peace through His blood, shed on the cross."

What is God doing in and through you now to renew and reconcile all things back to Himself? God has a mission for this world and He has a people for His mission. If you are His disciple, He has a place for you in His mission to rescue and renew. We should talk through our stories in such a way that others in our community can help us see what God has in store for us.

When you go back to your story's beginning, the good news, and discern how He made you and why He made you it can lead you to a longing to be restored back to your true form. "What no eye has seen, what no ear has heard and what no human mind has conceived — the things God has prepared for those who love him — these are the things God has revealed to us by his Spirit" (I Cor. 2:9,10).

Listening to Hear

One of the things missing in many curriculum-based discipleship approaches is that they do not take the time to learn one another's stories. Learning our stories together is an important link in the steps to enjoying life with God and others. We need others to help interpret our story and that is best done in a loving, confidential community.

> *"God accomplishes this work [of change] as the Holy Spirit empowers people to bring His Word to others. We bring more than solutions, strategies, principles, and commands. We bring the greatest story ever told, the story of the Redeemer. Our goal is to help one another live with a 'God's story' mentality. Our mission is to teach, admonish, and encourage one another to rest in His sovereignty, rather than establishing our own; to rely on His grace rather than performing on our own; and to submit to His glory rather than seeking our own. This is the work of the kingdom of God; people in the hands of the Redeemer, daily functioning as His tools of lasting change"* ("*Instruments in the Redeemer's Hands,*" Paul Tripp).

It is one thing for you to tell your story, both the good news of how God made you and the bad news of your ruin and alienation, but it is another thing for friends in C.R.O.S.S. community to listen, ask good questions, and respond. French psychologist Paul Tournier wrote, "It is impossible to overstate the immense need that people have to be really listened to and to be understood by another person" (*A Place For You*).

You must treat your discipleship time as a conversation and not a training session where one person as the subject matter expert teaches the others. It should involve asking questions, being curious, and responsive. It means that as one speaks the others listen, observe, respond, interact, offer insights, support, encourage, and sometimes give direction.

Gospelling Life Together involves intentional gospel conversations with focused discussions about one another's Relational, Personal, Missional, and Spiritual life so that each disciple loves, matures and reproduces — by the Spirit's power — the way God intends. It is at a most basic level sharing in life with others where each intends to connect and understand one another's story (their Backstory, how Christ has and is rescuing and discovering what mission the Spirit intends for each to be a part in the renewal of all things).

In the early stages of your C.R.O.S.S. group you will need to work harder on developing the connection. If you do, it will pay off later as trust and personal life connection are important. Learn one another's story. Let them know your story — all of it, wins and losses. Know them. Know their story. Hear how God made them and when they first began to think about why they were here. Listen and help interpret how their ruin and alienation set them on a self-directed course in life. Really hear them and God will use you, through community, to help strengthen, provide hope and hopefully, wise interpretation of how He is working in their lives.

Connecting With One Another

In a C.R.O.S.S. community, whether you are in a triad or quad, consider talking through the four aspects of one another's lives. Stimulate learning one another's gospel story; their good news, bad news, and very good news. Remember, your friends don't need you to fix them, but they do need you to love them deeply. It is fascinating how often all of us tend to substitute other things for the grace God has offered us in his Son Jesus. We all would rather contribute something and what a healthy C.R.O.S.S. community can do is help deconstruct those substitute attitudes and actions of contribution.

I was about 10 minutes into one of our meetings and while confessing a particular failure of mine and berating myself for being so stupid and careless one of my friends replied, "That is a gospel issue Tom. You are so self-righteous and think too highly of your own righteousness and as a result are being hard and condemning on yourself. I know you learned that pattern long ago, but come back home to the cross and find rest."

Now, I have been in other groups in the past where I would have never allowed anyone to see my failure, much less confessed it as such. In those environments, people pretend and close up.

The Relational aspect is where margin in life is given for people, in friendship, celebration, and community. The disciple's relationships with others includes: service to others, family issues, how they relate to a wife/husband, with children or with parents. It involves healthy conflict resolution. One of your friends may sense this area in your life needs growth and change. The other members can help diagnose the situation and help clarify the learning process needed to work the reality of the gospel into this area of life.

The Personal aspect focuses on a disciple's understanding his or her identity in Christ: How they handle their finances, physical fitness including mental and emotional and social wellness, time management, or academic pursuits. Work-life balanced with appropriate margins and life rhythms. As you learn each other's story you may discern this to be the area of life needing gospel empowerment and application.

The Missional aspects of a disciple's life deal with knowing God's love for sinners. It understands God's call for us to be light and salt in the world. It includes personal calling; the investment of time, energy, and money for the Kingdom; leading in local ministry. Your work matters to God. For many disciples this will require loads of discussion, trial and error and prayer. Engaging not-yet believers with the good news, bad news and very good news of Jesus Christ is extra-challenging.

The Spiritual aspects deal with our worship and praise of God and our belief in His promises to do good for us. He is our love, joy and adoration with all of our heart. It is our prayer, Bible study and meditation, and our worship of God by dedicating our time, resources and skills to His glory. It is practicing rest in the gospel.

"It is important to understand that fruitfulness and growth are the results of focusing on Christ and desiring to honor Him. When growth and change are our primary goals, we tend to be preoccupied with ourselves instead of with Christ. 'Am I growing? Am I getting any better? Am I more like Christ today? What am I learning?' This inordinate preoccupation with self-improvement parallels our culture's self-help and personal enhancement movement in many ways. Personal development is certainly not wrong, but it is misleading — and it can be very disappointing — to make it our preeminent goal. If it is our goal at all, it should be secondary. As we grasp the unconditional love, grace, and power of God, then honoring Christ will increasingly be our consuming passion...The only One worthy of our preoccupation is Christ, our sovereign Lord, who told Paul, 'My grace is sufficient for you, for My power is perfected in weakness.'"
("*The Search for Significance,*" Robert McGee)

Going to church is an important part of our growing toward maturity, but addressing our spiritual blindness, confessing our idolatry and need for God's Spirit to enliven us in a learning community with trusted fellow idolaters is life changing. The way we change is by changing what we worship.

Questions to Get Community Going

As you invite others into a C.R.O.S.S. community one of the first seasons of the group is to spend time in one another's lives. I would discourage you from jumping into a prescribed book or study materials.

Even if you plan to use a curriculum-based resource, spend time engaging with one another on a personal and meaningful level for a time where you begin to know one another and sense the trust building. The study books or other disciple-making guides will only increase in their effectiveness in bringing about the desired growth to the degree that you understand the people you are co-learning.

The following questions are meant to help initiate the conversations. They are not interrogation questions! As each of you answer, ask follow-up questions. It is not the time for you to interrupt to tell your stories. One person volunteers to go first and the other two being to interact with the questions in connecting and learning one another's stories.

Do not rush these first times. Be more interested than interesting. In other words, let each one talk about their experiences and answers. Learn to listen and ask connecting questions. Ask ordinary follow up kinds of questions of curiosity.

Relational type questions:

- Where did you live between the ages of 10-12 years of age? Did you live with parents? Siblings? Extended family?

- What was your first job? What do you love to do now? Is it with your mind, hands, or arms?

- Who is one person in my early memories that brings the most warmth to your thoughts?

- Who are the 5 most influential people in your life and why?

- How old were you when you first felt relational alienation?

- Describe a relationship in your past in which it has been hard to practice forgiveness.

- When or what was it in your life when looking back now you can say, "That was not the way it was supposed to be?

Personal type questions:

- What story did you hear as a child or early teen that captivated your thoughts, imagination and dream of your future? It may be a window into me understanding your life story now.

- What did you do during the summer breaks from school?

- Describe a time in your life when you said, "This is what I was made to do".

- What positive messages did you hear in your life? Name as many as you can up to seven.

- What kinds of things did you do for fun this past month? Is it what you like to do?

- What in your story makes you say, "This is the way things ought to be!"

- What are three things that you do well? You do them better than other people.

- What are five talents God has given you?

- What story did you hear as a child or early teen that captivated your thoughts, imagination and dreams of your future? It may be a window into me understanding your life story now.

- What is one thing about your personality that you wish you could improve?

- If you had the power is there anything you'd change about yourself?

- Name three of your biggest losses in life. How do you see those events shaping your heart?

- When is the whisper of the enemy (the lie that God is not there for you) the loudest in your ear?

Missional type questions:

- Describe what you did for your first job? How old were you?

- What do you love to do now? Is it with your mind, hands, arms?

- What feels hard to do — it's your "daily grind"?

- What life mission do you feel you are on?

- What types of things have others invited you to do or kinds of people you've been asked to serve?

- How have you engaged in the lives of not-yet believers in your sphere of influence?

Spiritual life type questions:

- Name three or four defining moments in life that affected who you are.
- Who were some people who had a spiritual influence on your life?
- What age were you when they were influencing you?
- What does prayer mean to you?
- Where did Jesus Christ come into your life to rescue you? How does he rescue and renew you now?
- What are three things you would like to change spiritually in your current season of life?

Chapter Seven

What You Do in C.R.O.S.S. Community

"We've climbed up mountains higher
than were ever in our hopes and plans.
We've held onto each other's hands,
Watched miracles unfold together.
And we've crawled on our hands and knees
Through valleys cold and dark and deep.
Sometimes not even sure if we could make it out alive together.
And if it wasn't for God's mercy and His grace,
There's no way we would be standing in this place.
But because He has been faithful,
Every step along the way,
Here we are together, together."

"Together," Steven Curtis Chapman

Gospelling Life Together means we have to get together. The complaint of many pastors is that people in the church today, though they claim they want community, are not willing to make time for it; not really deep community.

If one of the ways the Spirit God works the gospel down into our lives, into the motivational structures of our hearts, is through other people then it serves to our health to make time. Maybe, just maybe, it is not that people don't really want community, but we in church leadership have not really made it about community or friendship. We have made small groups or life groups more Bible study than friendship or life.

We do live in a hectic world. I suspect you are busy and do not make margin in life for the extras. However, we all do what we love to do. We all have the same amount of time each day. The person who says, I do not have time to meet with a few other Christians for C.R.O.S.S. community is really saying, "I have other things I value more than that right now."

Maybe they are good things, such as work, being with your spouse and kids. There is no point in appealing to your will by hitting you with the "discipleship rule." Using fear or shame to make you do what is to your own good defeats the purpose of gospelling life together. If you are still skeptical about getting into a discipleship community, I simply appeal to you to re-read Chapter 1, but also think about loving God in a non-traditional form.

For the first half of my disciple life I was taught a western, traditional, linear view of Christianity. We were taught that a growing disciple worked hard to get his or her priorities in line. I was told the prioritized life was "God first, Church second, wife and kids third, job fourth, and you last."

Later, another leader had reduced it to "JOY: Jesus, Others, and You." The leader's challenge was to look at your schedule and see where you were spending time so you could determine what you were really living for or essentially what you really loved. Now there may be some truth to it, however, it is overly simplistic to think that life is a list. It is more complex and holistic.

Jesus was asked, "What is the greatest commandment?" In other words, what is the priority for life? He replied, we are to love God and to love our neighbor. They are not in sequence. It is not love God for a certain amount of the day and then love my neighbor. It is do them both and do them together all the time.

We were made to orbit life in Him, and loving Him means to love others. I love God and am loved by God and when I love my wife as Christ loved, I am loving God. When you love others by serving them, practicing mercy, hospitality and justice, you are loving God. We love God by exercising our bodies and minds; by doing our jobs well (not working for man but as unto the Lord); by kids obeying their parents; by being witnesses to non-yet believers that Jesus Christ is a living savior; by worshipping God in singing, baptism, sharing in communion and prayer; or by connecting with other people in Church in community. Life is orbiting around the Relational, Personal, Missional, and Spiritual aspects of one another's lives.

For those who have come to realize that a way to thrive as a Christian is through the power of community and want a fresh way to do that this chapter will help guide you through the "what we do" in C.R.O.S.S. community. There are certain factors that can facilitate deeper relationships. One-on-one disciple-making is better than no disciple-making and historically most churches and para-church models have set it up that way. I would suggest it is limiting in its effectiveness and is not the best form of community. Tim Keller says,

"The chief way which we should disciple people (or, if you prefer, to form them spiritually) is through community. Growth in grace, wisdom, and character does not happen primarily in classes and instruction, through large worship gatherings, or even in solitude. Most often, growth happens through deep relationships and in communities where the implications of the gospel are worked out cognitively and worked out practically-in ways no other setting or venue can afford. The essence of becoming a disciple is, to put it colloquially, becoming like the people we hang out the most" (Center Church).

What is a C.R.O.S.S. Community?

There are a few group dynamics that serve to grow us in community and one major dynamic is group size. A C.R.O.S.S. Discipleship Community is not a small group of 10-20 people that meet in someone's house or third space for fellowship, bible study, prayer, and missional ventures. Those groups are very important and most churches practice small groups, missional communities or are themselves a house church. Nor is it a one-on-one relationship.

A healthy CDC is comprised of a group of men or women that meet as a "Triad," a "Fearless Fours," or a "Fab Five." Anything larger than 5 people will hinder not enrich deep community.

I happen to be an advocate of the triad. Think about the Triune God in all of eternity, loving and being loved by one another. The Father, Jesus Christ, and the Holy Spirit form a perfect community in Triad. Jesus began his disciple-making plan by selecting 12 potential leaders. In every list in the New Testament there are four groups of three listed. For instance, we are all aware of Peter, James, and John.

Those three did a lot of things together. Philip, Andrew, and Nathaniel are another triad who are frequently mentioned being together. I am not suggesting that it's the biblical way, but it does afford us with closer relationship and practically it can make it less likely one of you will skip out.

Triads, Fearless Fours, or Fab Fives are the best way to grow in a community. No one person is in the superior role. We are co-learners, co-confessors, and co-participants. There is also the dynamic of removing the natural barriers of race, class, ethnic, and economic status, etc. because in the gospel those dividing walls are gone. We are brothers and sisters, one new ethnic people. We can model that better in a three, four or five than one-on-one though I do believe you should use gender-specific groups.

In his book *"Transforming Discipleship,"* author and professor Greg Ogden, a disciple-making specialist, suggests, "As an alternative to the one-on-one model I propose a threesome that I call a "Triad" as the ideal size for a disciple-making group. Triads provide the setting to bring together the necessary elements for transformation or growth to maturity in Christ." I heartily agree.

C.R.O.S.S Discipleship Community enlarges our lives in knowing and loving God (Personal Aspect) in sustaining spiritual formation by the renewing of our minds, presenting lives as worship (Spiritual Aspect), in forming Christian community by living lives of love (Relational Aspect), and becoming transforming agents of God's graciousness in the city, region and nations of the world (Missional Aspect).

Most CDCs begin with a 10-12-week commitment with each weekly meeting lasting about 2 hours depending on the group size. You can plan for each member having about thirty minutes for each

gathering. The "when" and "where" is determined by each group.
The CDC can be done in person or if time and distance is a problem you can meet using Skype, Google Hangouts, or some other online service that connects visually. Since you are already related from your church and today's culture accepts digital group format as a normal way to connect with someone you can make the best of it. In 2005, I developed the C.R.O.S.S. conversation as a tool for gospel coaching. It has been used effectively in the U.S.A., Australia, Canada, Mexico, Cuba, and a host of countries in Europe. I think it also has landed in China. It is an easy to follow and natural approach to having an intentional conversation with someone. It applies easily to gospelling life with others:

C.R.O.S.S. community involves intentionally gospelling life with others through focused discussions about one another's Relational, Personal, Missional and Spiritual life.

Each discipleship conversation follows C.R.O.S.S. **(Connect, Review, Objective, Strategy, Supplication)** as the way we gospel life together.

Connecting: We connect RPMS to each other's current life, season, Backstory, and story.

Reviewing: We check in with one another on how God is working in us, and how progress or change is occurring in our life, based on the growth objective we set. Some have also called this section their "reality check," asking one another how they are really doing.

Objective: Each disciple sets a growth or learning objective in one RPMS.

Strategy: Each growth objective should have at least one strategy that is designed to be specific, measurable, aspiring (Jesus has to work), realistic, and completed in a given time frame.

Supplication: All our times together must include praying with and for one another. God must work. We need faith, repentance, and power. We, as a community of worshippers, worship Christ in our prayers.

Each member gets about 30 minutes to share what he/she is learning. The other two members are interacting with the him/her, connecting, reviewing, exploring life or learning objectives the disciple has made and thinking through appropriate strategies that move them along the journey to maturity, and praying with and for one another (total of 30 minutes).

Your friends do not need to be fixed. That is not the main purpose of gospelling life together. Love covers a multitude of failures and setbacks, but it also invites and prompts us to lay down our lives in pursuit of the highest good.

Organic Approach

An organic approach expects that whatever information and ideas need to work themselves into a person's life, values, and behaviors are developed primarily by the individual and worked out in the community. This approach is individually focused on each member working on their own unique growth plan based on their story and how they see God working in them.

This approach is learner-directed, with each disciple being intentional in his or her own growth plan. This is more than a few folks sitting around the coffee shop sharing what they have been reading, confessing how they have messed up that week or talking about what sermon they recently heard. This is organic, but is very intentionally focused.

One member may sense the need to grow in Relationship with his/her spouse and set a specific objective: "I will love my spouse more deeply the next six months."

Another may want to grow in Personal aspect of generosity and set as their growth objective "I will demonstrate practical ways of being generous with my time, my money and my things."

Another member may want to grow Spiritually in their knowledge of God or some bit of theology or develop a prayer life that engages God and want to grow by learning about the character of God.

Another may choose a Personal aspect like "I will lose 25 pounds this year." Our physical and mental health is vital to enjoying life with God and others, as we noted in the Core Disciple Identity (Chapter 3).

You could use the other concepts of the Core Disciple Identity or the RPMS of C.R.O.S.S. Discipleship Community defined earlier. All may want to discuss the verses and concepts of our identity in Christ and decide that that each needs to be involved missionally in the lives of others and create individual or group engagement in mission with strategies for prayer, sharing the faith and serving in mercy and justice issues.

The idea is that each is personally involved in their own learning, and the others are involved in accountability, prayer and support, offering ideas for growth. As one takes on a learning or growth objective others may add their ideas for strategies to achieve that objective.

For instance, deciding what books or podcasts can you point them can help with forming strategies. Who can they interview or interact with further to grow and mature? What timeline will they be on? How will they apply the implications of a radically changed heart to their growth objective instead of relying on their own will and duty?

Unified Curriculum Approach

A unified curriculum approach calls for a prescribed set of information and ideas to be downloaded into a person's thinking, values, and behavior. The preferred curriculum in engineered discipleship is material that explains the Bible and applies it to the details of our lives. You can use the same book all together. That would depend on where each of members of the group are in their respective journeys or where they want to go together in their journey. It might be that your home church has a book study they prefer everyone participates in and you can incorporate C.R.O.S.S. community into that unified curriculum.

Whichever approach your group decides to adopt we must remember at the fundamental level all of us have been called, as His disciples, to be witnesses of His resurrected life. We are to be living as Missional disciples who have been set on this course by Jesus himself. There is no way around that.

We are not simply to meet together for our own personal benefit. Our spiritual growth is to thrive the way God intended and His intention is for His glory, His very own goodness displayed through Jesus to be made manifest to all His creation, through us individually and corporately.

As I've noted before, God has a mission and He has a people for His mission. He will renew all things. That is where Gospel Story is heading. In a C.R.O.S.S. Discipleship Community there are two ways the conditions are set for mission.

1. You help discover what is the mission God has you on. It can be exciting for you to be in a community with some other men or women older or younger so God can speak to and through them, be helped to discern areas you personally need to grow in grace and mission. No two persons are made the same or experience the same needs or issues at the same time.

2. Together you go on mission. Plan to be in mission together or perhaps join another triad in mission.

What is the mission God has you on? You may answer, "Tom, I'm retired. I did my bit at church and at work and raising my kids. I'm done now."

Ok, I get the sense one feels that they did their leading and mission already. But God is still on mission to renew all things. There are some men or women only a few years behind you that can both speak into your world and where you can, God willing, speak into their world.

In the book "*Gospel Coach*," Scott Thomas and I wrote,

> *"Since we are in Christ, we have a missionary identity. We are adopted into a missionary family. We serve a missionary God. Mission becomes part of our identity, because our Father is a missionary God and we resemble him as a child of God. So, the Church is a missionary church, with missionary people, that do missionary things for the glory of a missionary God. It is who we are and it is also what we do. Mission is not something we tack on to the list of options as a Christian. It is what we are commissioned to do and something we must commit ourselves to pursue with all of our abilities. Mission is not just something we do, but something we are...Gospel Coaching facilitates transformation through realignment in the Gospel."*
> ("*Gospel Coach,*" Tom Wood & Scott Thomas)

We must never omit Supplication in our C.R.O.S.S community. Prayer is not just an added phase to conclude your C.R.O.S.S. community. Sometimes prayer is necessary during the conversation. It isn't necessary that it waits until the end. Sometimes we should stop and confess sin or praise God for granted grace and forgiveness. Sometimes we may stop and offer praise and thanksgiving for the great things God has done.

At the end though prayer allows C.R.O.S.S. disciples to realign the focus and dependence upon the gospel and His Spirit. Ample time should be reserved for praying together.

Being a disciple of Jesus is a spiritual work, unlike the working in a business venture or charity. Whenever we see the work of God advancing we will see opposition. The great enemy of God and the Church is watching, hovering, plotting and scheming in various ways to keep us from growing healthy.

The Spirit is how we appropriate the gospel of grace into our lives and ministry because it is His role to point us to Christ and the work of the gospel as all-sufficient. We must remind one another that by the Spirit the gospel has given us a new power not only to know and desire God's will but to do God's will (Phil 2:13). It will be by the Spirit applying the gospel that we will continue to grow in grace (Rom 5:5; Gal 5:22-23), to minister in confidence despite personal weakness (2 Cor 3:5-6), and be bold in mission (Acts 4:31; 7:54-60). "All God's work in us, touching our hearts, our characters and our conduct is accomplished by the Spirit" (Richard Pratt).

If the time is rushed at the end of a session the temptation is to speed through the prayer time. I have found that skipping it or rushing through prayer diminishes the influence of our relationship and we lose out on the prayers of our small community.

What Needs to Change?

What are the basic elements for a transformed life? I suspect most of you are trying to have an approach to disciple-making or spiritual formation that is more organic than formulaic. I'm with you on that. However, to be truly organic does not mean less intentionality, but more. It means that when we gather together as communities of lives being changed into the likeness of the perfect human, the True Man (human), we have to agree as to what that looks like.

Just to be clear I do not mean we are all lookalikes. We are not photocopies of Jesus Christ. He is the eternal God, we are not. He did not become God by some great act, like His baptism or the endowment of the Spirit. He is and always was God the Son. But He was born a human being and He remained the perfect man.

We are each unique and talented humans. Being a Christian, a follower of Jesus Christ, does mean that Christ through His Spirit is shaping us in the four aspects of life to become eventually fully human. It does mean that we can and do overcome the damages of our sinful choices and actions, as well as, the guilt and shame sin has done to us. We cannot change our past but we can change the future of where that past takes us. We have freedom from the enslavement of our sin, both present and past.

We have been saved and are being saved from this world from the evil one and from our own selfishness. And that is best done in the loving friendship of a discipleship community of others who pray with and for one another, who care deeply for the good of one another, and who can speak the truth in love to each other.

> *"God's gracious provision for our needs includes God's grace for sanctification as well as for justification. It is not enough to tell believers, 'You are accepted through your faith in Christ'. We must tell them also, 'You are delivered from the bondages of sin through the power of the indwelling Christ.' Even if we are assured that our sin is covered, we do not want to face the despair of having to live in the conscious helpless awareness of its tyranny, abusing the grace and forgiveness of Christ."*
> ("*Dynamics of Spiritual Life,*" Richard Lovelace)

What does it mean to be a Christian Relationally, Personally, Missionally, and Spiritually? And what does the gospel call us to change into the likeness of those aspects in our ruined or alienated lives? Again, what are the ways of the transformed life?

RELATING (Arms)

Jesus said once, "Love one another. As I have loved you, so you must love one another. By this all men will know that you are my disciples, if you love one another" (John 13: 34,35). Francis Schaeffer, a deeply spiritual writer, philosopher, and missionary to the unbelieving generation of the 1960 and 70's, entitled a talk and booklet on this passage, "The Mark of the Christian." We can't spend the extensive material given in the Bible on how the gospel is to change us relationally, but I encourage your discipleship group to tackle this one.

It could take you one full year of learning to get through the one hundred times the Greek word, "Allelon" (One another) is used in the New Testament. There are common commands to love one another, to be at peace with one another, serve, devote ourselves to, accept, forgive, and submit to one another (just to name a few).

There are many stories Jesus told regarding how we are to relate to one another. Community is the core of our being yet it has been ruined. But the gospel is the power for community renewal, racial reconciliation and relational healing.

One of the things I regularly told our congregation when I was a pastor was that I prayed and worked hard among them so the watching world would look at us Christians and say, "I have never seen a group of people love the way you guys love. We have never seen people forgive the way you guys forgive. We have not seen blacks and whites care together the way the people at your church care."

If we ever did get there (and we did more than we didn't) it was because we knew we had been so loved. We were intentionally and generously obeying the Lord's command to love one another so others would know we were His disciples.

KNOWING (Head)

There are things that disciples of Jesus have to know. Once I start the list, someone reading will say, "he left off," and then name some other things we Christians need to know. Rather than make a long list of things we must know, can we agree that our heads and brains do have to get engaged in following Jesus? "Be transformed by the renewing of your minds" (Romans 12:1).

Maybe in your C.R.O.S.S. community you could spend some time listing the things you think Christians will have to know about God: the Bible, Gospel Story, nature of humans, and other theological realities like being justified, sanctified and glorified. What you believe (know) or don't know about Jesus will make a huge difference in how deep a faith you will have. Developing a theology of suffering or justice will only deepen our lives.

I had just shared Gospel Story with Mark, a friend of about two months. He accepted that there was a God and that God had revealed himself in the Bible and that God the Son had come to the earth, lived, died, and was raised to life.

I asked him if he wanted to turn his life over to that loving God and rely on Christ for life instead of his own self-efforts. He said "No." "Why not?" I responded. He said, "I understand that if I become a Christian I will lose the direction of my own life and have to follow His lead. I do not know who Jesus really is or how reliable He is to turn control of my life over to Him."

I asked him if he would get with me and Bob, another man in our church, and begin reading the gospel according to John so he could "know" Jesus. The Apostle John wrote that one of the reasons he wrote his gospel was so "you may believe Jesus is the Christ and know you have eternal life" (John 20:31).

DOING (Hands)

Here is where many of young disciples today "spill their milk." They wrongly assume that being a Christian is only about being in an existential way the experience of being loved and accepted. There are skills such as teaching, administration, wisdom, giving, etc. that we are called to all be involved in.

All disciples are specially gifted by the Spirit to participate in the life of the local church as mutual servants of grace. The New Testament gives remarkable clarity on the fact that every disciple has been given at least one spiritual gift to use in the maturing of other believers in the church and for missionally engaging our neighbors.

BEING (Heart)

Again, New Testament scholar Richard Lovelace helps us:

> *"Only a fraction of the present body of professing Christians are solidly appropriating the justifying work of Christ in their lives....Many...have a theoretical commitment to this doctrine, but in their day-to-day existence they rely on their sanctification for their justification...drawing their assurance of acceptance with God from their sincerity, their past experience of conversion, their recent religious performance or the relative infrequency of their conscious, willful disobedience. Few know enough to start each day with a thoroughgoing stand upon*

*Luther's platform: you are accepted, looking outward in faith
and claiming the wholly alien righteousness of Christ as the only
ground for acceptance, relaxing in that quality of trust which
will produce increasing sanctification as faith is active in love
and gratitude"*
("Spiritual Dynamics," p.101).

Conclusion

A man once told me he was jealous of my disciplined life and that he could not be that way himself. It was during the most challenging time of my life.

I almost laughed as I said, "I appreciate your suggestion that I am a disciplined man. I'm not. I am lazy. My desk proves my disordered life. But self-control, the self-management we need for life, is not a matter of the will but of the heart. We subordinate our lives to the thing that is most important to us. We are always controlled by what captivates our heart. As I have suggested elsewhere, 'whatever takes our breath away.' Most mornings my prayers seem irrelevant and shallow. But the men and women who have traveled this life before us have told us if you want God you have to seek Him even when He's silent. And my dear friend, God has been very silent these last months. Let's keep encouraging one another in the story God has."

The ancients of our faith have told us that there are regular ways that the gospel is pressed down into our hearts and lives to take hold of us. They include worshiping God, both personally and with others; reading, memorizing, and having the Bible taught; praying to God; participating in Communion; and being in a community of other believers.

Your C.R.O.S.S. community will, to the degree you traffic in the gospel — as you gospel dance, interpret one another's gospel story — will be a deep place for honesty, transparency and joy. When you can't find the deepness it is probably because you abandoned the gospel and some rules based accountability system has taken root. If you go back to grace, your fellow passengers on the journey will help you see the hidden things in your heart and help guide, pray, exhort, and encourage you to begin the process of motivational change.

The writer in Hebrews 3:7-19 reminds believers to "fix your thoughts on Jesus" because we are the "house" that Christ built, but also warns against two things: Not to doubt and not to disobey God. "See to it, brothers, that none of you has a sinful unbelieving heart that turns away from the living God. But encourage one another daily as long as it is still called Today so that none of you may be hardened by sin's deceitfulness."

A university campus worker related a personal story to me about meeting with a co-ed to discuss what her roommate's beliefs about Christianity were all about. The philosophy major had never heard about Christianity, other than small stories about weird churches.

The campus worker began by telling her the Backstory: there is a God who made all that we see and made us for good and with dignity. We were made with beauty and wonder to know and be known. But our first parents didn't believe God wanted their good. They wanted to be their own gods, so they committed cosmic treason against God and His clear instruction. Because God is just and true they were put under a curse of death. But God is also a God of love and He came himself, God the Son, to take away the curse by becoming the Cursed One. He was put to death for our treason and rebellion against Him and was buried.

At that moment the co-ed yelled, "Stop. Just stop! You mean to tell me that your god is dead? Seriously, what a total waste of time! Do you know how many religions have dead leaders?"

My friend responded, "Just wait. Yes, Jesus Christ was put to death and was buried, but three days later God the Father raised Him from the dead and He is now alive."

Every day we need to remind ourselves and one another we are disciples of a living, risen Savior who is able to do more than we could ever think or imagine in our little minds. Start a C.R.O.S.S. Discipleship Community and get going in the plans God has for you.

Chapter Seven

Chapter Eight

Inside a
C.R.O.S.S. Community

"We're all broken. And we all need a Savior. This is a fool's parade. The way we masquerade. Trying to make everybody think it's all okay. When the truth is we're all living a story. What if we all got brave, Enough to take away? All we're hiding behind even for just a day, And let the scars show even a little, But I know the honesty will show us all to be. We're all broken. And we all need a Savior. We don't have to pretend about it. We don't have to keep acting like we're all okay. If we lift our eyes to the cross. We'll see the reality."

"Broken," Steve Curtis Chapman

If we were in a retreat or a super Saturday workshop for C.R.O.S.S. (Connect, Review, Objective, Strategies, Supplication) Disciple-making, one of the activities you would do is break into triads and work through the C.R.O.S.S. conversation with your fellow participants.

For now, let's sit in on a C.R.O.S.S. community group meeting. Of course we cannot write out a two-hour conversation, so it will be excerpted. However, you will get a taste of what it might look like.

Having said that, one leader asked me if I would give him a script for his group. He has four, high capacity leaders that are gospelling life together and they are very different. I told him I could not, nor would it help.

The approach is to be self-directed. Let the participants decide how far and how deep they will go. We can use starter questions, but the group will take its own direction.

The following C.R.O.S.S. Discipleship Community example is made up of three men:

Pete is a natural born leader, married to Trish and has one daughter. He is very driven and owns his own successful business with over two dozen employees. He loves Jesus a lot and has shown loads of leadership ability in the early stages of a young church.

Jon has been married to Liz for about two years. He is more a lover than a fighter, but he, too, is a solid young emerging leader. He grew up with a lot of traditional religion and has become very interested in the Christianity that is based on God's kind grace rather than his good works.

Jim is the oldest of the three and knows the Bible and theology well. He and his wife, Marta, have been both leaders and Bible study teachers in their previous church. He is careful and wise.

Pete and Jon are close friends that hang out together and their wives are friends. They both have known Jim for a while.

They all attend a new church and formed a C.R.O.S.S. group because they each wanted to follow Jesus in a more intentional way. All three are committed to personal change and to the mission Jesus Christ called them. They have been meeting formally as a group for almost eight months, but they also get together other times as well, working on mission projects with the church's service days and attending several baseball games.

The first time they met they decided to spend the first several meetings just talking about their own personal journey in life, and not rush into any type of formal study. They used a handout sheet from a Men's Retreat on Gospelling Life as their guide for learning one another's story.

Questions on the worksheet were designed to promote the telling of each other's Backstory to better learn how God had rescued them, and what path He had for each in the renewal of all things.

Pete had stated early on that he was not interested in getting together so they could "fix" him. He wanted friendship with other men and that meant they would do more than have home groups or read books or be accountability partners.

"I want a group of guys where we don't pretend to have our act together, but we know we can't keep doing life on our own," said Pete.

Below are a sampling of questions built around the four aspects of life. These were the questions they used to get their group life going, in addition to the questions at the end of Chapter Six. You can use them and see how deep your group can get just by taking the time to listen and be interested in your friends' lives.

Relational Life

- What did your dad do for a living when you were in high school?
- Who was one of your favorite teachers? Why?
- Who are you married to and how long? How many kids and what are their ages?
- What are some of your key relationships currently in life?
- Who are you most responsible for in life?
- Who can't live without you or you without them?

Personal Life

- How often were you sick as a child?
- What is the purpose or meaning of your life right now?
- Name 3 or 4 defining moments in life that affected who you are
- Name a few hobbies you would like to do that you don't have time for right now.
- What would you be willing to give up if you were promised the best of the best life?
- Who is tending your soul?
- What things do you do now that brings you the most pleasure? What frustrates you to no end?
- What are two habits you'd like to overcome?

Missional Life

- What was the best job you ever had?
- What is your main interest in the marketplace?
- How did you first realize your world wasn't way it was supposed to be?
- What is your current business role and how do you see it as a fulfillment of what you were made to do?
- What types of things have others invited you to do or kinds of people you've been asked to serve?

- What work or marketplace responsibilities do you have that you enjoy? What ones do you hate?

Spiritual Life

- If you could ask God one question what would it be?
- Where do you believe the world came from and where do you think it's headed?
- If you were raised in a Church, what kind of messages were you given in terms of being a Christian?
- *One thing is absolutely certain: if the Gospel doesn't take your breath away, something else will.* What kinds of things in this world take your breath away? Good, bad, beauty, ugly...
- Can you name any people who had a spiritual influence on your life?
- When did God become more than a nice concept to you?

Pete, Jon, and Jim meet weekly, taking turns gathering in one another's homes. When they meet, they spend time Connecting with one another over coffee or a cold drink or sometimes a quick meal.

Each takes about ten to fifteen minutes talking about one of their four aspects of life. It takes about thirty to forty-five minutes to get through their Relational, Personal, Missional, and Spiritual connection because they are so close.

With that done, they then move on to their Review time. We will pick up the meeting at this part of the group and I will use excerpts of their meeting so you can catch a glimpse as we go inside.

Pete: *As you guys know, for the last few months, I have been working on a mix of personal and spiritual struggles with self-control. Sometimes when the words are coming off my tongue, I wish I could get them back. I can lose my cool and it gets me into trouble.*

Jim: *Anything happened recently that you want to talk about?*

Pete: *Just this week, one of my top guys made me so mad. I wanted to chew him out for being so stupid. I held my tongue because I don't want to lose him, but man I was mad. I made a few comments to him, but nothing like what I was thinking.*

Jim: *Which is worse, the bad words or the bad attitude?*

Jon: *You mean we have to pick? Ha. Ha. I think you are a jerk all the time, but I am used to it.*

Pete: *Very funny. Jim, I don't know. Maybe it's both.*

Jim: *Maybe you haven't thought deep enough about it. Do you think it's wrong about losing your temper or saying bad words or is there something deeper going on beneath the bad words?*

Jon: *I remember reading recently, Jesus said, what comes out of the mouth is from the heart and that's what ruins us. It is what is in your heart, the inner self, that's what comes out of us. I know you could blame it all on your dad. Your backstory is filled with unhappy memories of your angry dad. But what about now? About three months ago, you were going to try a new approach. What have you done so far with the ideas we explored?*

Pete: *Well, I have been listening to a guy on podcast every day when I am on working out. I listen to music when I am doing weights, and a sermon when I'm on the treadmill and elliptical. Some of those messages have hit home. I also have watched a few youtube videos about anger management.*

Jon and Jim: *That is great to hear! Anything else?*

Pete: *I am trying to listen to Pastor Jake's sermons at church and talk about it with Trish. I've read the Bible too, but honestly not that much. And I do have a brief prayer time with God while I'm on the throne. Ha, Ha!*

Jon: *You're an idiot.*

Jim: *Well, I think its great you are focused on changing your temper. Remember what we read in the Gospelling book and materials we studied about changing? When we repent, it has to go deeper than the* *expression of sin, but to the reason or motivations? When you get angry, do you ask yourself the "why" question?*

Pete: *Yes, and that is making a lot of difference. I really don't want to lose control.*

Jon: *So, where does Jesus have to show up now in life? As we say, what is the present value of what Jesus did for you?*

Pete: *One of the podcasts I listened to, the pastor said, "Your emotions are like lights on the dashboard of your truck. When the red light goes on you'd better not stick tape over it and hope its nothing. Instead, let the light make you check out what is wrong. When you lose control, its not enough to just say, ok, don't be mad or ignore the fact that I am angry. What I am learning to do, is stop, ask God to show me why I am getting angry and once I can see what is driving me—typically its because I am being inconvenienced somehow—I can say to myself, I need to act in love, and cussing someone out is not loving them they way Christ loved me and gave himself for me. The pastor suggested we use the Bible to help us so I memorized some verses from that I try to think about every day.*

"So, chosen by God for this new life of love, dress in the wardrobe God picked out for you: compassion, kindness, humility, discipline. Forgive as quickly and completely as the Master forgave you. And regardless of what else you put on, wear love. It's your basic, all purpose garment." That's from the book of Colossians, in The Message.

Jon: *I think Paul says, just before that, that we are to put to death or put off the things that were how we used to live- like anger, cursing and lying. Stuff like that. Then we are to put on the new. It would be like me going to the gym in the morning before work and getting all nasty sweaty and then just putting on my polo and black jeans over the gym clothes and going to work. That wouldn't make any sense. I have to take them off then I can put on my work clothes. I think what you read is really good stuff. I think if we would memorize and think about those verses all the time it would help change us.*

Jim: *Maybe Jon and I should memorize those verses too. We can say them to each other each week! I mean I know there is a lot in my life I need to quit doing and stuff I need to start doing. We have to learn to speak to our own hearts because I have the most influence on me than* *anyone. I talk to myself all the time. Thanks Pete. Can I talk to God about this right now?*

They stopped and each prayed, realizing of their own lack of love for others, and Pete asked God to work powerfully in his life to believe that Jesus is his life and through that, control himself when he gets discomforted. Then, the conversation continued:

Jim: *So, Pete, what is next for you over the next few weeks? What do you think some next steps are given what you are already learning about self-control?*

Pete then gave some new ideas for his learning path toward self-control, a character quality he wanted to see develop into a richer and deeper part of his life. Next, the conversation continued on to Jon:

Jon: *Well as you know, Liz and I are still learning how to be married. We are really growing well. She is definitely a stronger personality than me, but we are adjusting. I thought the first year of marriage was hard, but we are still figuring it all out.*

Pete: *How much time have you had with her in the last week?*

Jim: *You said your aim was to spend daily time with Liz, to connect and deepen your lives. You mentioned several things you had planned to do...dating her once a week, cooking meals at home together and other stuff that's necessary for a happy marriage.*

Jon: *We are following the advice about going out on a date once a week. We have to set a time because we are both so busy that we are rarely home on the same nights. She works late three nights, goes to the gym a couple of late afternoons and has bible study one night. We are together at our small group but that isn't the same.*

Pete: *Seems like you made a nice duty list, but is there something else?*

Jon: *Well, it's hard to admit this (tears begin to fill his eyes), but some stuff came out about her and her old boyfriend that I didn't know about and it ticked me off. I haven't decided what to do about it yet.*

Pete: *Man, that stinks. I am sorry. I don't know what to tell you. No matter how hard it is, God will take care of you and her. Love covers a lot of junk.*

Jim: *I want to pray for you and Liz. Take it from an old married guy, no amount of anger or climbing into your man cave and pouting will solve it. Let's ask God for strength to deal with the hurt and fear. It is good you can acknowledge it. That took courage.*

Jim's prayer focused on Jon's fear and need for hope. Jon managed to say a short prayer for God to help and give him faith and love.

Pete: *So man, how can I help?*

Jon: *I don't know. You can't fix this. Just knowing you care...that's good. Maybe we will need to talk to someone. Is Pastor Jake good at this marriage stuff?*

Jim: *That sounds like a good idea. Do you think Liz would go and talk to him too? Or would that be weird to ask her to go talk to the pastor?*

Jon: *She is pretty private. I don't know. But I will ask her.*

It was evident that Jon did not want to go any deeper or discuss any more of the issues regarding his marriage. Jim and Pete both knew it was time to move on and did not want to force anything. Obviously, he had shared with them more than he had intended and they knew it was time to stop to discussion. They thanked Jon for his honesty and told him they would be asking God to help him in making good decisions and learn to love even when it hurts.

Jim's turn was next. Both Pete and Jon were a little intimidated by Jim at first, but after several months, they found it easy to talk to him about their lives. He was a lot funnier in their group than around church. Pete was also a pretty forward person so he was not afraid to take the initiative.

Pete: *What have you been doing lately with your neighbors? I know you are trying to figure out what mission God has you on in the renewal of all things.*

Jim: *Yes, that was a great question you asked. I care more about myself than the not-yet believers in my life. I have been teaching bible studies for Christians for years and years. I know my theology. But I realized that I have never seen anyone come to a believing faith in Jesus Christ for their salvation. So many people I have taught tell me their salvation stories—or their Gospel Story as we have been studying. But I have not had the joy of leading someone to believe the gospel for the first time.*

Jon: *Hmmm. Pete have you ever led someone to see Christ as Savior?*

Pete: *Besides my kids, only a couple of guys in my fraternity back in those days. It was amazing to see someone come to faith in Christ and watch their whole life begin to change. But no, not since then.*

Jim: *I've never introduced someone to Jesus and it grieves me to say so. I know I need to repent of it and it is because of God's kindness and mercy toward me that makes me want to ask God to forgive me for my lack of love for the not yet believers.*

Jon: *Why does it bother you? It seems that God has used you in other ways of teaching Christians theology and stuff. I mean you and Marta are so open with your home for bible studies and stuff. Isn't that part of how God made you, to be a teacher?*

Jim: *Thanks for the encouragement. Yes, I do think God made me and then gifted me to teach. I guess what I am seeing now is that teaching isn't an end to itself. Teaching people about Jesus and the gospel should take us to his mission. I'm realizing I missed that along the way. Our new church has reminded me of our call to be missionaries in our own neighborhood's and in the marketplace.*

Pete: *If Jesus were to ask you, "What do you want me to do for you?", what would you answer?*

Jon: *I can answer that. Make my marriage better.*

Jim: *Wow, I have never thought of that. Hard to know the answer, right now. Can I think about it and get back to you?*

Pete: *Of course.*

Jon: *Jim, What is one most significant contribution of Missional influence you want to use at our church?*

Jim: *I want to change the way I think about the people around me. I don't want to be so judgmental. I can be critical of other people's views about God. Instead of caring about them I want to argue my case with them. I want to have more love than the certainty of truth. I don't want to stop living with truth, but I want to love more. I think that will be huge diff for me. People in need, need for mercy, need for God's love, all of that, I want that to change in me.*

Pete: *That is amazing.*

As I mentioned, all we did was to sit in on excerpts of their group time. We have to remember that they spent months getting to know each other well enough to talk plainly with one another. Even with that, they also had issues that were private and, as in Jon's case, unwillingly to deal with at the moment. That is fine and good.

In other venues of disciple-making, that issue might have never even come out. So, even in this meeting they did not try to fix anything, they were able to talk about it later and ask about it. And, Jon and Liz are still very happily married. Jon felt the sting of shame early on, but had the courage to walk into the pain and darkness of not knowing and become the man God had intended.

Some of you reading this may think there is little reality in what you read. In fact, you would not ever see yourself having that level of life with a couple of other men in this world. That says more about the current condition of our churches than you. We were made for community and through that shared relationship, can interpret our lives and learn the hope we need to become what we deep down, in the deepest part of our being, know we were meant to be.

Conclusion

Gospelling Life Together does not have to be complicated. You can keep it simple and not be simplistic. However, you do have to be intentional in your relationships. For the group to work well, there has to be a destination. Change is inevitable because we are constantly exposed to new ideas, new sorrows, new stimulants and new people.

For good change to happen, you will need to commit yourselves to the relationships in a C.R.O.S.S. group for a season. I don't know how long that is. You will need to determine that together. You will also need to decide to serve others outside your group.

Being on mission together is a value in and of itself, because living a generous life is what it means to know grace. It also will build trust and love among the group. Sitting around, working on ourselves is not the call of the gospel. Jesus did not die to make you nice, but New. Being made New takes you somewhere. Get ready to go!

Appendix: Case Study Kings Church, Long Beach, CA

Pastor Jason Mather took the *Gospelling Life Together* material and adapted it to his own context, using language that was consistent with their own vision as a church.

Instead of calling the groups C.R.O.S.S. Discipleship Community groups, he changed it to Cluster groups.

Since they used "Upward, Inward, Outward" concepts in their mission statement he wanted the members to see their groups as an UP, IN and OUT format.

The purpose of including Kings Church Long Beach as a case study is so you can see that Gospelling Life Together can be adapted to any church context and will facilitate disciple making relationships.

Cluster Groups

Purpose:

To provide an intimate, intentional and supportive environment for people to grow in their relationships UP (Spiritually), IN (Personally) & OUT (Relationally & Missionally).

How Long: 12-week sessions – each weekly meeting lasting approximately 2 hours

Who: Three Men or Three Women

Where & When: This will be determined by each group.

Why:

"The "why" of discipleship is the good news of the gospel. We disciple because God has discipled us personally through Jesus Christ. In fact, God sent his only Son to follow him when all of us refused. Rather than crush our rebellion, Jesus voluntarily took our place by humbling himself and learning obedience through suffering. Out of God's great love for us, he transferred our sin – past, present and future – onto his only Son. Jesus offers us his righteousness and inheritance, which should inspire awe in the heart of every believer. We have been so loved, forgiven, instructed and empowered! We must tap into the gospel motivation of why we do what we do each time we meet together (Dr. Tom Wood)."

What:

We view Cluster groups more like an "independent study" environment rather than a class where the learning objectives and materials are predetermined by a professor. Each participant, with the help of the other group members, will select one to three objectives to focus on during the twelve-week session. We recommend choosing one goal for each area: UP, IN, & OUT but some may prefer to limit their objectives to one or two.

For example, Mike, Jim, and Sam have decided to start a cluster group. Mike wants to spend more time studying God's Word so he picks, as his UP goal, a devotional study on the Gospel of John. Jim realizes that he isn't sleeping enough so his IN goal is to average 7 hours of sleep each night. Sam wants to be a positive Christian witness in his workplace so his OUT goal is to pray for his company & coworkers during his lunch break once a week.

At each Cluster meeting, Mike, Jim, and Sam will share how they are progressing on the objectives they have set for themselves UP-IN-OUT. The group also has the freedom to pick the same goal(s) that everyone will pursue. For example, the group may decide that all of them need to lose 10 pounds so that may be the group's IN goal.

Example objectives

UP (Spiritually)

These learning objectives should help cultivate a growing relationship with God. The spiritual disciplines, such as studying God's Word, prayer, meditation, fasting, etc. will often be helpful objectives to pursue but do not feel limited to only the traditional disciplines. How would you like your relationship with God to change? What changes can you make in your life to make God more of a priority?

Examples:

> - *I want to read one book on the attributes of God*
> - *Each week I want to listen to one sermon on God's love*
> - *I want to pray for ten minutes before bed at least five times/week*

IN (Personally)

These objectives should focus on any area you want to grow personally. It may be related to your physical health, hobbies & interests, finances, education, habits...whatever area of personal growth you want to pursue. How would you like to develop as a person? What would you like to be different about you one year from now?

Examples:

> - *I want to learn how to play golf by taking a weekly lesson*
> - *I want to listen to the audiobook "Gilead" by Marilynne Robinson*
> - *I want to attend one conference on parenting*
> - *I want to sign up for an exercise class*

OUT (Relationally & Missionally)

These objectives should always be "other-focused." Think about the people in your life and the current state of those relationships. Is there something you would like to change about your relationship with your parents, spouse, kids, or neighbor? Where are you investing your time and energy in serving others: your family, church, and community?

Examples:

- *I want to take my spouse on a date night twice a month*
- *I want to invite three people to church*
- *I want to read "The Art of Neighboring"*
- *I want to wake up earlier so I can be "ready" when the kids wake up*

Tips for a Successful Cluster Group Experience:

1. Try to set objectives that are measurable. For example, perhaps you want to get out of debt (IN goal). Quantify that goal with a number: "I want to decrease my debt by $2,000 by the end of twelve weeks."

2. Don't compare the size or difficulty of your objectives. This may be hard but you shouldn't feel bad or self-righteous about your objectives. Each person's objectives are significant and should be encouraged & celebrated. We're not competing against one another. We're simply trying to grow as individuals in a community setting.

3. Be positive and supportive with one another in pursuing your objectives. For example, one of your group members has a goal to spend 10 minutes a day reading Scripture at least 4 days a week). How should you respond if she doesn't reach her goal that week? Here's how the conversation might go:

You: "So...how did you do this week with your UP goal?"

Her: "I read 2 times this week."

You: "Ok, why weren't you able to reach your goal for the week?"

Her: "I was lazy...I forgot...life is crazy right now..." (Fill in the blank)

You: "Is there any thing we can do to help you reach your goal this week?"

Her: "Yeah...maybe one of you could send me a reminder text in a few days?"

4. Sometimes the conversation will lead you away from talking about objectives...that's OK. This is "life on life" discipleship meaning that sometimes you just need to address whatever important issue is going on at the time. The objectives are important but not the most important thing. Be open to where the Spirit leads the conversation.

5. We are developing relationships that involve invitation and challenge. In other words, we're inviting one another into our lives...to see things that others don't see. But we're also giving one another permission to speak into our lives, challenging us to follow Jesus faithfully. Invitation and challenge is a difficult balance to strike but it is essential to a successful group. Vulnerability is required from each participant.

6. We can't fix one another. That's the Holy Spirit's job. You can offer input but you have to let go of trying to force it down someone's throat. Offer the input and than let go it (give it to the Holy Spirit to use as He sees best).

---

7. Listening and asking good questions is the best place to start when engaging with one another. This will be THE key skill to develop to make these groups effective. Not easy for most of us since its much easier to jump to the answer or solution instead of really trying to understand one another and the particular circumstances.

8. What is shared in the group stays in the group.

Overview Of The Twelve-Week Schedule

There are several dynamics involved in a cluster group experience. The first priority is to understand one another's story.

You will spend the first three weeks taking turns sharing your story (see the section below titled Sharing Our Story) and listening to your other group members. Listening well and asking good questions with a desire to know and understand one another will be the springboard for a successful group.

On week four, after each participant shares, you will offer your UP-IN-OUT objectives, allowing your group members to give input if needed. Then, the remaining meetings will follow the C.R.O.S.S. format suggested in the section below.

The C.R.O.S.S. format is a suggested structure for your group meetings. C.R.O.S.S. stands for Connection, Review, Objectives, Strategies, Supplication.

This 12-week schedule and format is just one way a cluster group could be done. If your group develops a different approach please let the pastoral staff know (it may be a more effective outline for other groups as well). Your feedback during this process is essential for making cluster groups a fruitful part of our church life.

12 Week Schedule

1 Preliminary Meeting with a Pastor to go over these materials

1st Week – One group member shares his/her story followed by questions & prayer

2nd Week - One group member shares his/her story followed by questions & prayer

3rd Week - One group member shares his/her story followed by questions & prayer

4th Week – Each member shares their UP-IN-OUT objectives with discussion & prayer

5th Week – C.R.O.S.S.

6th Week – C.R.O.S.S.

7th Week – C.R.O.S.S.

8th Week – C.R.O.S.S.

9th Week – C.R.O.S.S.

10th Week – C.R.O.S.S.

11th Week – C.R.O.S.S.

12th Week – C.R.O.S.S.

———

Sharing Our Story

A key element of the Cluster group experience is sharing your story and understanding other's stories, in light of God's greater story. How has God designed you, what experiences and relationships have impacted you positively and negatively, how is God working in your life and using you in the lives of others.

We suggest that you spend the first three weeks taking turns sharing your story with one another. No one should feel forced to share any personal information they're not ready to share. We've included questions to use when sharing your story. Also, leave plenty of time for your group members to ask you questions.

59350208R00089

Made in the USA
Columbia, SC
02 June 2019